The Lost Art Of Direct Sales

By Edward Harding

The Lost Art of Direct Sales.

Copyright © 2011 by Edward Harding.

All Rights Reserved.

No portion of this publication may be reproduced, stored in a retrieval system, or transmitted by any means—electronic, mechanical, photocopying, recording, or any other—except for brief quotations in printed reviews, without the prior written permission of the publisher.

Editor: Joshua D. Lease / Aegis Editing / www.AegisEditing.com

Cover Design: Bill Greaves / Concept West / www.billgreaves.com

For information about special discounts on bulk purchases, please contact Edward Harding at P. O. Box 2189, Capistrano Beach, California, 92624, 1-888-511-6827.

Library of Congress

ISBN 978-1-4507-3902-3 soft bound
ISBN 978-1-4507-3903-0 hard bound
ISBN 978-1-4507-3904-7 ebook

Published by Bush Publishing / www.bushpublishing.com
Printed in the United States of America

Testimonial

Ed Harding has been my mentor for the last 26 years. By following his Seven Steps of Successful Selling and being a diligent student, I went from a loser to a multi-millionaire. What worked for me will work for my organization, so I've just ordered copies of his book for every member of my sales team.

If you don't believe me, try it yourself!

Alan Jacob, **CFO**

Digital Dolphin Supplies

Dedication

This book is dedicated to my beautiful wife, Paula. Without her help, support, and love this book would have never been possible. She has worked tirelessly to help me complete it. My heartfelt thanks and love go out to her.

Contents

FOREWORD
  By Tony Robbins vii

INTRODUCTION xiii

CHAPTER 1
  Sales is a Profession, Not a Job 1

CHAPTER 2
  The Psychology & Language of Sales 9

CHAPTER 3
  The Structure of a Sales Presentation 23

CHAPTER 4
  Sales is an Art: The Introduction of Creativity 31

CHAPTER 5
  The Seven Steps of Successful Selling........................41

CHAPTER 6
  Handling Objections 69

CHAPTER 7
  Closing the Sale 97

CHAPTER 8
  Advanced Closing 129

CHAPTER 9
  Recruiting and Training: In Order to Keep it,
  You Have to Give it Away 139

CHAPTER 10
  The Philosophy of Successful Selling 145

CHAPTER 11
　　Setting Goals 149

CHAPTER 12
　　The Art of Selling Creates Money:
　　What Do We Do With The Money? 153

THE LAST WORD
　　By Gerald Chamales 171
　　You Can -- If You Believe You Can

CONTACT INFORMATION 175

Foreword
By Tony Robbins

You Never Know What's Going to Change Your Life Forever

For me it came when adversity intersected with an advertisement.

It was 1977, and at the time I was a seventeen year-old boy attending Glendora High School in Southern California. I was a committed student who wanted to be a professional athlete but understood his limitations and had adjusted his dream and refocused on becoming a sports writer or a sportscaster. I had my whole plan in place. I was doing well in school; I had worked for a local newspaper; and would qualify for a scholarship to USC and go on to be involved in the sports world covering the extraordinary athletes who inspired me.

But, it wasn't meant to be. I'm the oldest of three, and to say my mother and father had a volatile relationship would be the understatement of the decade. Their fights were quite physical, and finally, on Christmas Eve in 1977, they hit a peak of violence that led to my father destroying pieces of furniture and storming out of the house.

Shortly after, when I spoke up and defended my father, I was the next one to go. Unfortunately, my dad had already taken off—I had no idea where or how to reach him. There were no cell phones in those days, and my father was not the type of person to leave a trail.

I found myself walking through the rain on Christmas Eve with nothing but the clothes on my back. My mother kept my 1960's Volkswagen that I bought by saving $40.00 a week as a janitor while I was still attending school. So, I found myself staying in the laundry room of a friend that night and trying to figure out what I was going to do with my life. Sparing you the gory details, it's sufficient to say I found myself in a unique situation.

I was seventeen; I was attending high school. I had virtually no income. I had no savings, and I needed to support myself immediately.

What changed my life? Looking for a job, I turned to the want ads and spotted one that appealed to me. It simply said, "Make $500 a week as a Manager-in-Training" with three keywords, "No Experience Necessary." Thinking I was clearly management material—$500 a week, or $2,000 a month could give me an incredible lifestyle. Being fully qualified—with no experience necessary—I decided to immediately apply for the job.

It was no surprise when I arrived at the interview that there was a group of fifteen or twenty people all waiting to apply. Rather than go through the traditional process of individually interviewing people, this organization decided to try a different approach. They told us that we would have a group interview initially with the founder of the company, an extraordinary man named Ed Harding.

Before interviewing us, he gave us an overview of what this special music company was about and what the management opportunities could bring.

When Ed entered the room, I was completely in awe. It wasn't just that he was dressed impeccably, but it was his sense of presence: a passion that sparkled in his eyes and a sense of absolute certainty and confidence that you rarely experience from another human being.

He walked through the room of mismatched applicants, and when he sat down he launched into a presentation about what it would mean to become a professional, what it could mean if we could learn the art of persuasion, to become professional salespeople, to become masters of influence. He made it clear that it would not only help us to earn an unlimited income, but in the long-term, it could influence the quality of our lives and help us to touch others as well.

There was something about the man that was so unlike anyone else I met before that I was captivated. He told the story of his own life, of how he had been an alcoholic, how he had lived with such fear, how he lacked the fundamental confidence to take on any real challenge in his life, and how this profession transformed him. And now, as the owner of the company, and as the manager of salespeople from all over the country, he had created an exceptional lifestyle, not only for himself, but for those that he loved. He offered for those who could make it through the tough training process to show us how we could do the same.

Then, before he spun and jumped into his stretch-limousine to drive away, leaving us with a group of sales managers to do the interviews, he said that there's one thing you have to be certain of in this job—you're only going to be paid what you're worth, so you better find a way to serve and add more value than anybody else does.

I was hooked. The idea of being a person of influence, someone who could touch lives, who could get people to do things that no one else could get them to do, to get them to follow through, and to be able to test my own mettle really appealed to me. I wanted to discover what I was really worth, and it excited me to no end. I applied and was accepted into the most intense training program ever.

Day and night I immersed myself into the training process, which you'll learn from Ed in this book. There were tools that I learned from his mentor, one of the original great influence teachers of the last past half century, J. Douglas Edwards.

I listened as he talked about how nothing in business mattered—the economy actually stopped—unless someone could influence someone else to take action. I extrapolated how this could be used to help me influence myself to take actions to get through my own fears and shape my own life.

During my first week out after total immersion I had pure hunger and absolute passion. I went out to represent this company, which at the time sold cassette tapes. Yes, I'm ancient enough to remember a time, far before iPods—even a year before the famous Sony Walkman came out. To this day, music is a huge part of my life in my seminars as a way to shift people's emotion, psychology, mood, and movement.

I loved meeting people in their homes and connecting with them, understanding what their needs were, overcoming their fears and objections, and giving them something I really believed in. There was just one problem. I lost the laundry room to stay in and was now sleeping in my 1968 Volkswagen. I literally had no money, and I decided to go on a dietary "fast"—primarily because I literally had no money!

I arrived on the final days excited and knowing I was about to get paid because I had exceeded the records for sales! But instead of a celebration, Ed and his team were very grim. They pulled me into the back room and said, "There's something we need to teach you about sales; it's called buyer's remorse." I didn't get the education to find out that while people bought in my presence, maybe they didn't stay in state and changed their mind later on. As a result, none of my sales had gone through.

Ed said, "But you're a really good salesman. What can I do for you?" I said, "Feed me." So, that night, they took me to Denny's, and I ate everything on my plate…and theirs too! <u>But I stuck it out,</u> and I decided that selling was more than about making money; it was truly about understanding the most important skill of life: <u>how to lead</u>.

If you're a person who's interested in learning to lead, both yourself and others, if you're a person who would like to not only have an unlimited income—where you're paid to add value—but also where you can learn to manage others and get leverage and expand yourself as a business person, then I can't recommend more highly the teachings of the man who I'm indebted to for providing me my first job and my first exposure to the fundamental rules of influence. And that is my dear friend, Ed Harding.

At the age of sixty-seven, he has built dozens of companies and is a multi-millionaire many times over. He has plenty of property, a magnificent wife, and beautiful children. His lifestyle is outstanding, from golf to yachting. But what I can tell you about Ed is that he's the real thing. He's a man whose passion, hunger, and vision to constantly grow and be better has never left him in the forty-plus years of his professional life.

Now, at this stage, he's decided to put together a book on the lost art of direct selling to share with you the insights he's learned over four decades of contribution. I can tell you that at its core, he'll teach you the most important and fundamental psychological principles and techniques of influencing. But behind it all, techniques will not work unless you understand that motive does matter.

I really believe that Ed's success, along with his skill, is his pure intent. He's the man who spent decades helping others and sharing with people how to become professionals in the field of selling simply because it opened up an opportunity to a young man lacking confidence who was in deep pain. It provided for him not only a lifestyle, but a way of helping others to increase their quality of life as well.

I have many privileges in my life today. But whether I'm working with the president of a country, a company, a top-athlete, a financial trader, a mom, or a person who is suicidal—that capacity to step into someone else's shoes, understand what they deeply need and sincerely find a way to serve them is still the fundamental process that guides me. And even to this day, the seven master steps of influence that you'll discover in this book are a part of my unconscious design whenever I'm getting up to speak to influence someone for theirs and other's greater good.

I can still remember over thirty years ago being mesmerized as Ed taught us those same seven skills every week, one after another, with that same passion, with that same enthusiasm, with that same sincerity, with that same hunger and commitment. Most of us want to learn new things that are exciting, but fundamentals of service and of influence are skill sets that will serve you as long as you live no matter what profession you're a part of. And if you are considering sales as a profession, I just want to let you know that you're about to meet the mentor who touched my life deeply, a man I now get to call my dear friend, Ed Harding.

Enjoy the journey. I hope our paths meet someday and that I'll get to hear how my dear friend, Ed, touched your life as he touched mine. I wish you great challenges, extraordinary growth, and magnificent levels of contribution to yourself, to your family, and to society.

Live with passion.

With love and respect,

Tony Robbins

Introduction

I am sixty-seven years old. I have spent forty years in the sales business, most of it in training. At night I sit, and, just as a matter of curiosity, watch infomercials. I am curious to see what is being sold. Many infomercials are about health and body building. Others relate to beauty and skin care. Many claim to teach people how to make money, attain wealth, or achieve their personal goals.

I am really interested in this latter group.

As I listen to these gurus tell people how they can make more money and become more successful in real estate or some other area of acquiring money, I ask myself, "Will these ideas really work?"

Invariably the answer is, "No."

Most of these get-rich-quick infomercials are really pie-in-the-sky. They might work for one in a million, but for the vast majority, they are not reality. In fact, I have even seen infomercials displaying a disclaimer that pops up in the middle of the screen that says, "Most people who purchase this program do not make money."

As a result, I have been thinking. What could help people make more money and realize that they might be standing in their own acre of diamonds right now?

What evolved is the idea that if people possessed a set of tools that *really worked*, they could start improving their lot in life immediately! By using and mastering these tools, they could elevate their positions as entrepreneurs or become more successful in the endeavor in which they are currently involved or employed.

What right do I have to tell people how to become better entrepreneurs and succeed in business? I will give you the short story. At twenty-seven years old, I started out as a door-to-door salesman. When

I knocked on my first door, I was so negative that I was actually thinking, "I hope there is no one home."

After that early experience, I began to really study the profession and learned that selling is a combination of guts, perseverance, and psychology—all three operating at once to make the prospect sitting across from you *want* to own your product.

As my professionalism and production increased, I reached the point where I set the goal that I wanted to be *number one*. I, indeed, became the top salesman in my company. Most importantly, I discovered that while I could accomplish 100% through my own efforts, if I trained ten people to do 50% of what I did, I would add 500% to my production!

I became top manager, then regional manager, then national sales manager. I was making more money than most people could even imagine! Next, I had to learn how to invest that money so that the money, itself, would produce. Over the course of forty years, I went from starting with nothing—driving a 1957 Desoto that had to be started with a screwdriver—to my state in life today where I have a net worth in the mid-eight figures.

I hope I can convey some of this information and wisdom to you and assist you in discovering your own acre of diamonds.

Edward J. Harding

"An American Sales Champion"

Chapter 1

Sales is a Profession, Not a Job

Most young peoples' first or second job will often involve some type of selling. For example, they may begin working in a retail store, fast food restaurant, department store, or any number of other positions that involve interaction with customers. In my case, my first job was a paper route. After seeing the evolution that has taken place in the delivery of information, I am not even sure paper routes exist anymore.

In the nineteenth century, a young person's first job might have been shining shoes on the street corner. Today the young people going out and getting their first jobs selling a product or service to a customer may think they've got a lowly, humble job that will carry them through while they go to school or decide on their real career goal. Here is the critical point where these young people make their first mistake: They do not realize that the delivery of a product or service to a customer is actually the humble beginning of entering the highest paid profession on earth!

Make Your Vision Your Reality

Sales is a profession, not a job. In fact, these young people with their timid "Can I help you, sir?" have actually entered the highest paid profession on earth. One of the reasons that people don't realize the significance of their first opportunity is that it is not taught in schools. In our almost completely dysfunctional educational system, as you progress from kindergarten to graduate school, you are never even likely to hear of sales being referred to as a profession, much less being taught as part of the curriculum. But I will say it again: the fact is that sales is the highest paid profession in the world!

I cannot emphasize this strongly enough, nor can I repeat it too many times. No other profession exists that gives people the opportunity to create their own success or failure like sales. Picture in your mind what your life could be like in the next ten years. You can make your vision your reality through sales.

Most of the population does not realize that salespeople are the thoroughbred racehorses of every corporation. Without the sales force, nothing moves by truck, by train, by boat, or by plane. There is nothing on the shelves of any store; there is no food in supermarkets; there are no medical supplies in hospitals—need I say more? In fact, the leaders of every giant multinational corporation to the owners of every small business have all sold their product. The reality is that without sales, not only does nothing move, but the company will create no revenue to pay the vast number of employees from bookkeepers to secretaries to laborers of every sort. The point is that the paycheck for every job is a result of the salespeople that sell the product. It's a fact that sales are responsible for every dollar created by every enterprise on earth.

> **Salespeople are the thoroughbred racehorses of every corporation.**

Pay Your Dues; Reap The Rewards

Just like a lawyer, doctor, engineer, accountant, financial analyst, marine biologist, or any profession you can name, a salesperson is exactly the same—a highly-skilled expert. The professional salesperson will have spent several years studying and mastering the profession of persuasion. The big difference is that in every business, the top salesperson is a big shot, someone to be consulted, a master of influence, and someone whom others seek out for thoughts and methods to emulate. I cannot tell you how many times I have heard an employee complain about the incessant demands or unbelievable arrogance of a salesperson…only to hear the boss reply, **"Remember, without him you don't have a paycheck."**

Speaking of bosses, when I went to work in sales in 1969, I was very fortunate to have a great mentor named Joe Martin. He taught me the profession. One of the reasons I mention this is that in today's world of celebrity, fame, and star-struck teenagers, people look for role models or mentors in the wrong places. Instead of giving them good direction, these so-called "mentors" automatically set them up for failure. When I started selling in 1969, my first goal was to make $300 a week. By 1984, I was making $60,000 to $70,000 a month. I didn't know many doctors, lawyers, or engineers who made more money! If you use money as a yardstick for success—which is wrong-headed thinking to begin with—then by that yardstick, I had already reached the top of my profession.

> **If you pay your dues, you can reap any reward that your mind can conceive.**

I feel that the real definition of a successful person is someone who does what he or she wants and loves to do, and, consequently, receives the type of rewards he or she emotionally needs. For example, a great schoolteacher or nurse is not looking for the same kind of reward as Donald Trump. So when I say that sales is a profession, I guess what I am really saying is that if you pay your dues, you can reap just about any reward that your mind can conceive—which can be anything from money to redemption. A lot of really hard, merciless businessmen who have walked over others to get to the top of the heap become philanthropists in order to redeem themselves. This being the case, when I see people saying, "Buy my book, and I'll show you how to get rich quick," I find it offensive on every level of

Edward Harding

consciousness that allowed me to reach out and actually experience greatness.

Start With The Basics

Let's begin by laying out a very basic curriculum that an intelligent person of any age can study in order to become a true professional. I think the first and most important part of an education to become a professional salesperson is to buy a copy of Napoleon Hill's *Think and Grow Rich*. For those of you who do not know the history, Napoleon Hill was actually the first person to start teaching success and motivation in sales. Napoleon Hill was the first modern motivational speaker and the founding father of the entire modern motivational movement which includes some of today's greatest motivators such as Tony Robbins.

I actually gave Tony his first job. He dropped out of his senior year of high school when he was seventeen to work for me because he said that he thought he could learn more from me than he could in high school. I would say he made a good decision and then took action on it. He was almost eighteen, and his mother was so angry that she kicked him out of the house. For a couple of days he had to sleep in his car until we could arrange some living accommodations. (By the way, Tony is about 6'6" tall, and his first car was a Volkswagen Bug.) I imagine it was hard to get a good night's sleep, but Tony was such a great salesman that he made money very quickly. I think in his first two weeks of production, he made about $900 in "1977 dollars." Tony and I are still friends today, although he has far exceeded my level of success. I am very proud to have been his first teacher as an entrepreneur and positive thinker. Tony's seminars worldwide have helped millions of people take their first step toward living their dreams. I suggest to everyone who wants to progress: attend Tony's seminars and read his books.

Back to Napoleon Hill: he was a young man who dropped out of law school for financial reasons. He began writing for small town newspapers in Virginia. He considered the turning point in his life when, as part of a series of articles, he interviewed Andrew

Carnegie. Carnegie was impressed with the young Hill and offered him the task of interviewing the top five hundred most successful people in America. The list included Thomas Edison, Alexander Graham Bell, George Eastman, Henry Ford, Elmer Gates, John D. Rockefeller, F.W. Woolworth, William Wrigley Jr., William Jennings Bryan, Theodore Roosevelt, William H. Taft, Woodrow Wilson and Franklin D. Roosevelt. .

When Andrew Carnegie gave this assignment to Napoleon Hill, he did not hire him nor did he give him a paycheck. He only guaranteed that Napoleon Hill would have access to these super-successful Americans, and it was up to Hill to make of it what he could.

He originally titled the results of his work *The Philosophy of Achievement* but in 1937 he wrote *Think and Grow Rich*, which is basically a study course in personal achievement and establishing a positive belief system. *Think and Grow Rich* is the sixth best-selling business book of the last seventy years, having sold over thirty million copies. All of today's motivational speakers and teachers of the philosophy of success still use Hill's works to expand their students' consciousness and help them establish a basic belief system. Hill died in 1970 at eighty-seven years old having influenced countless millions of people.

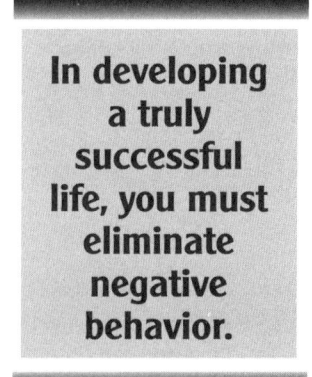

> **In developing a truly successful life, you must eliminate negative behavior.**

In interviewing all of these people, Hill found that each of these successful men had certain similarities in their thought processes. In other words, they all thought alike and had similar beliefs. It was for this reason that *Think and Grow Rich* was the first book I read when I started studying to become a professional salesperson.

As a funny aside, in *Think and Grow Rich*, Napoleon Hill explains what he calls the "thirty day test." In other words, if you can go thirty days without finding yourself overwhelmed by negativity, then you pass the thirty day test. If, at any time, you find yourself being controlled by negative thoughts and emotions such as anger, fear, resentment, jealousy, etc., you must go back to the beginning and start the thirty day test all over again. It really sounds very simple, but if you do it with rigorous self-honesty, you'll find that it is actually very difficult. It seems funny to me today that it took me fifteen years to really feel in my gut that I had passed the thirty day test. *Think and Grow Rich* is a textbook you can use to embark on the process of successful thinking.

After Learning To Think, You Can Learn To Earn

Next I recommend you buy and study every book on professional sales techniques. Read as much as you possibly can by every author who teaches positive mental attitude combined with the selling process. From Dale Carnegie to the *Psychology of Winning* by Dennis Waitley, many of these works can be accessed through the internet. For example, one of the greatest lectures I have heard can be ordered from Nightingale-Conant—*The Strangest Secret* by Earl Nightingale. This forty-five minute CD provides just about everything you need to know in order to progress on a daily basis. I listened to it years ago on tape in my car—over and over again—along with other sales training tapes like those by the greatest of all sales trainers, J. Douglas Edwards, who we will discuss in much more detail later.

> **"Action" is the Magic Word!**

Taking Action

Reading great books *begins* the pathway to success. But know that it is critically important that you, the reader, realize that reading all these books and knowing all this information is absolutely useless *unless you put it into action*! You must actually do what the teacher instructs. *"Action" is the magic word!* Without action and practice, you won't become really proficient at conversationally using many of these strategies. Take action now. Don't delay and you will begin to see the success you have always wanted.

Along the way you are going to find that sales is primarily a psychological process. But unless you **PRACTICE, PRACTICE, PRACTICE**, in order to be effective in your presentation, these tactics will appear *contrived*. Your prospect will know it immediately, and you will be out on your ear. The use of these sales tactics must be totally conversational. If you do not follow this instruction, you will not climb to the top of the hill.

That just about sums up what I have to say about sales being a profession except for one important thing. In developing a truly successful life, you *must* eliminate negative behavior, whether that negative behavior involves drinking too much or just being a gossip. In my case, I had a serious problem with alcohol. Even though I became the number one salesman by 1972 and was driving a brand new 1973 Cadillac, one night I had too much to drink and drove that brand new car right off the road into a construction ditch. So negative behavior will absolutely interrupt or end any progress you might make. It wasn't until I finally quit drinking in 1976 that I really began to grow into the successful person I wanted to be.

I recall a defining moment in my thought process. Shortly after I quit drinking, I thought to myself, "If I'm not going to drink, I might as well learn how to make money and live well." That realization ultimately resulted in being able to live in a manner that very few people are able to achieve. I'm not trying to intimate that I'm Donald Trump or Bill Gates, and really that was never my goal, but I do live a great lifestyle. In the summer I live at the beach and spend a lot of time on my boat, which is an 80-foot yacht docked right in front of my waterfront home. In the winter, from January through May, I live in the desert (Palm Springs area), which probably has the greatest winter season climate on earth. That covers the material side. I have a loving relationship with my wife; I have a great relationship with my children; and I practice God's presence in my life on a daily basis.

So all in all, I would say that sales, as a profession for me, has given me the ability to climb to the top of the world. Of course, there are always other influences or experiences in life that add to a person's evolution while becoming wise. You must be tough in business but fair to all people. If you learn to think, study and take action to be a professional, and eliminate negative behavior from your life, you have taken the first steps to mastering the greatest profession in the world.

These elements are part of mastering yourself. Your next step is to start understanding someone entirely different: your prospect. In the next chapter, I will show you how to become a professional at reading your prospect as well as the importance of the words you choose. If you are ready to make some money and become a master of influence, keep reading!

CHAPTER

2

The Psychology & Language of Sales

The most important strength of your psyche must be an attitude of *service*. This is an important chapter and is the second chapter for a reason. In this chapter we are going to create the basic platform of our selling mentality. When a salesperson goes into a sales situation, his or her state of mind is very important. In sales you have creative, artistic, and brilliant people who, in the space of an hour and a half, can meet a total stranger and overcome that person's discomfort of being under the pressure to buy. This pressure naturally exists in the sales situation regardless of whether the person is making a decision to buy a new pair of shoes or to buy a new home. In these situations, there is a tremendous difference and importance between a pair of shoes and a home, but as strange as it may sound, the feeling that your prospect gets is exactly the same. The only difference is the degree and intensity of that feeling.

Your sales prospect is automatically going to feel resistance. The professional salesperson's job is to not only overcome the resistance but also to eliminate that initial feeling and put the prospect at ease. This requires that the salespeople put themselves in the prospect's psychological position. In other words, psychologically trade places with the person you are attempting to influence so you can understand his needs.

You must also know and understand that the resistance your prospect automatically feels requires you to take the time to put your prospect totally at ease so you do not increase the discomfort of the pressure situation. In other words, you must make the resistance go away, even if only temporarily. This psychological "trading places with your prospect" goes on throughout the entire presentation. As a professional, you must learn to sense when it's rearing its ugly head. Even when you give a great presentation, you will find this resistance coming out over and over throughout the presentation. It's your job to recognize when and where you meet resistance and to be ready to put your prospect at ease at any given time.

> **The most important strength of your psyche must be an attitude of service.**

This is why I say, *"The professional salesman is also a great psychologist!"* Everyone is different—there are as many different types of people as there are people, and you will find that in all types of people, their own resistance or bias can present itself in different ways. In a sales situation, your state of awareness must be totally on alert. You must be able to recognize everything from eye contact to body language, and this will include even a quick glance between a husband and wife. You must be ready to read every expression on your prospect's face throughout your presentation, and you may be giving a presentation to a single person or a group of people.

Stick To The Script

Many salespeople do not stick to their presentation as they learned it. They change it. As a result, many times they have to think about what they need to say next, and while they are thinking, they may miss an important reaction from their prospect. Understand that when you are giving your presentation, you must know it like the back of your hand. You cannot take time to think about what you're supposed to say.

Every great professional will give the same presentation over and over and over again, thousands of times over a period of years without changing a line, just like a great actor playing a part in a Broadway play that runs for years. That great actor may miss a line or a cue while the audience may never know it. The actor knows when he has dropped a line or misplaced his emphasis, even if it is on a single word. This is being a professional. For example, if the professional golfer makes one bad swing or one bad putt, it can make the difference between winning and losing a tournament.

> **When you are giving your presentation, you must know it like the back of your hand.**

I am reminded that in the army, the first general order is, "I will walk my post in a military manner keeping always on the alert and observing everything that takes place within sight or hearing." Imagine what that requires of an individual—to be aware of everything that takes place within sight or hearing. That's quite an order! Now consider that your job as a professional salesperson is to have this level of attention and commitment directed to your presentation and your prospect.

In addition, the sales professional must constantly monitor his or her own internal reactions. Imagine being the representative of a giant manufacturer who builds airplanes. You are sitting with the purchasing agent for one of the large airlines, attempting to sell fifty jumbo jets for billions of dollars. The commission could not only support your family for two or three years but also enable you to make a great investment that would take care of you in retirement. Your internal positive state of mind will project on to your prospect…or your negativity can cost you the contract--which is certainly not the result you want to create.

The pressure goes both ways, but the professional salesperson has the advantage because he or she gives that same presentation over and over again, possibly several times a day, for many years. Even though the example that I use here is extreme—and this sale will not be closed in an hour and a half—it demonstrates the importance and the magnitude of a ***great presentation*** as opposed to a ***mediocre presentation.***

Are You Ready To Win?

You must answer an essential question: Are you going to become a great sales professional, or are you going to remain an order taker? That's the question all salespeople must answer in their own guts as they make the decision of how much time, effort, and persistence they are going to put into mastering the highest paid profession on earth, that is, leading and persuading people.

When you take inventory of your own mental attitude, you must ask yourself, "Are you ready to win?" You can read every book in the world, but only experience and practicing excellence will enable you to give that great presentation and facilitate the perfect interaction and communication between you and your prospect.

Your positive mental attitude is a critical factor in achieving excellence. That is why I mentioned in my introduction that the first time I knocked on a door I was thinking, "I hope they're not home." I was new, inexperienced, insecure, and to top it all off, I had a negative mental attitude. With that type of mentality, I had a zero chance of succeeding. In order for me to make the transformation from a loser into a winner, I had to make a full hundred and eighty degree change. I was definitely a loser destined for mediocrity.

Fortunately, I had a burning desire in my gut to pay the price to become the person I wanted to be. I remember everything that my mentor, Joe, taught me. One of the first things he said to me was, "You can have anything you want; you just have to be willing to pay the price." Fortunately for me, I was willing. I would probably be more accurate to say that I was humble, because for me the definition of humility is *being teachable*. I was not only teachable, I was anxious to learn and soaked up information from Joe and from many other sources like a sponge. I still do today.

It's important to note that any person striving for excellence must learn from a multitude of sources. All your information should never come from one source alone. Fortunately, I was blessed to have a great teacher. I was also willing to learn every lesson and had the guts to put these lessons into action. You'll find out it takes guts to try something new!

While I absorbed all of this information—and I mean listening to tapes from the time I woke up and showered and shaved, every minute in my car, reading books, and learning the exact techniques for handling various objections and closing sales—*none of it meant anything until I put all of it into action.* For example, I might have been trying a closing technique I just learned that involved a story such as the "Benjamin Franklin Balance Sheet Close" (we'll cover this close in detail in chapter seven). In order to use this close, you must preface it with a story reminding people of our great founding father, Benjamin Franklin. It required a brief history without being too wordy, but still the words had to be exact. The first time I attempted this rather sophisticated closing technique, I was very awkward, and I know I got it all wrong. As I kept practicing over and over again—I progressed to the point where I could lead into the "Benjamin Franklin Balance Sheet Close" while remaining completely conversational. In other words, the prospect would have no idea that I was setting him up for a closing sequence that, if used properly, is very powerful. When I fully mastered that

> **When I fully mastered that particular closing technique, I'm sure I added at least $10,000 a year to my income. Remember, those were "1970's dollars".**

particular closing technique, I'm sure I added at least $10,000 a year to my income. Remember, those were "1970's dollars."

The Psychology Of America Today

In order to complete my transition from 1969 on—and as I continue to grow even today—I had to constantly work on studying my prospect and knowing how he was thinking and reacting as well as maintaining my own positive mental attitude, which included visualization as well as communication. I think I have covered the psychological part on a personal level as deeply as I can in this chapter, and I can positively testify that these methods work if ***put into action.***

But it seems that I would be remiss if I didn't at least take a look at the psychology of America at this moment. In the United States today, it seems like our country has gone crazy. As a youth, I learned values such as the greatness of America, the Constitution, the Bill of Rights, the fact that we saved all of Europe from being conquered by Germany, all of Asia from being conquered by the Japanese, and saved billions of people from genocidal maniacs like Adolf Hitler. It is a fact that the second largest genocide of all time was when the Japanese invaded China and killed ten million people. If not for the strength and influence of America and those young men and women who sacrificed their lives in World War II, the world would be an entirely different place. *America has really never attempted to create an empire.* We have never conquered countries and wanted to enslave their people. We have spread opportunity and democracy all over the world. In fact, the entire world economy of the international market place is being built on the back of the American middle class. American values and generosity have lit up every corner of this planet.

All is not the same as when I grew up. Many critics out there hate the American ideal. They hate the class mobile free enterprise system where people can go out in the world and create whatever life they have the strength, the courage, and the vision to create. They want America to be equal with countries that currently can't even take care of their own people or their nation's most basic needs. I don't mean to sound harsh here, but it's true.

I truly believe that America has contributed more to the world than all of the other countries put together. Think of every invention over the last hundred years. How many of those inventions were invented by American ingenuity and built by the American worker?

Yes, the American work ethic has led the world. And yes, we have definitely shared our wealth. For the last one hundred years, the American middle class worker made the greatest products on earth and today is sacrificing many opportunities to create jobs in India, Japan, Taiwan, China, South America, and on and on. America's productiveness has been the light of the world.

> **We have created the greatest place in the world to be born, to live, to work, to dream, and to be free to design our own futures.**

Our Constitution is a divinely inspired document of the freedom of our Republic to be held up as an example for the entire world to emulate. When I think of the people who denigrate and apologize for our greatness, it makes me sick. The fact is that we have earned our greatness. And, of course, we don't want to turn the greatness of America into arrogance, but we should have influence on the economies of the world. We have sacrificed our own economy and jobs to build theirs, and we are doing so now. So when I think of the American salesman as a professional who has sold the greatest products ever invented in the entire world, it makes me proud to have been a part of it. And it humbles me that God gave me the gift of living in America.

Today the younger generation tells me that enrollment in business schools has dropped to an all time low; it saddens me. It seems like everything is backwards—up is down and down is up. Young people today do not want to be salespeople. Our educational institutions do not herald what is literally the highest paid occupation of all time. I hope that the young people going out today to create their own world will use common sense in making the changes our great nation needs.

The politicians tell us that social security is broke, yet every American worker has paid from every paycheck into the social security fund. The fact is that it has been *stolen* and put into the general fund to finance an entitlement society that became fat and lazy compared to the lean, hungry Americans who built this country into the greatest political and economic power in history. And this generation and those who come after will have to pay the bill.

When I hear that racism separates people rather than bringing them together, I must remember that the only color I can see is green. We are all human beings. And I know that those who forget history are doomed to repeat it. I don't mean to be politically incorrect; you can actually Google this for yourself. It's a fact that Americans did not sell Africans into slavery. It was Africans who sold other conquered African tribes as slaves. An unfortunate part of our history is that in the south, the African American became the energy source that fueled the economy of that period. But we have corrected our mistakes like no other country! We have created the greatest place in the world to be born, to live, to work, to dream, and to be free to design our own futures.

The American dream has been the role model for the world. Let's not lose it by spending ourselves into bankruptcy, losing our national sovereignty, and then apologizing for being an American. Let's not claim atrocities that we did not create. Unfortunately, we used the energy of slavery, but after a hundred years and straight thinking, Americans ended this horrible reality and even fought a civil war over it. What country or empire throughout history has been so self-regulating? We cannot lose this attribute. And along with the personal psychology of selling, we must also be aware of the overall psychology of our own country.

A Word On Commission

Speaking of income, any *professional salesperson worth his salt is on commission.* In my opinion, when it comes to sales, commission is the only compensation I would ever want. I want to get paid for what I produce. I believe that—particularly in sales—if you are not on commission, somebody is being exploited. Either the salesperson is exploiting the employer, or it is the employer who is exploiting the salesperson. In either case, it's a bad situation and must be corrected. Ideally, the more expensive product with the greater commission will definitely put a professional into a higher income level. And off the subject, I would like to add that when that professional trains ten people to do what he does, his income rises exponentially. More importantly, he or she will become a leader of other people. This skill is absolutely necessary to become a champion.

> **If you're not going forward, you're going backward.**

The salesperson on commission and striving for excellence is always learning. The rule is: if you're not going forward, you're going backward. Your choice of language and altering your vocabulary is something you can learn—and learn easily and quickly.

The fact is that there are some really nasty words that should never be used in a sales situation. I cannot emphasize strongly enough that eliminating the words I'm going to cover is critical. One mistake can change the entire direction of a successful situation or a successful sale. Remember, it's a game of seconds and inches. One wrong word can cost you your commission, so let's start out by eliminating nasty words that can destroy your sale. And by eliminating these negative words, you can begin to increase your income now!

Language Is Critical!

The *language of selling is extremely critical* and can raise your income immediately. Now we are going to enter the real field of selling. The language of sales is so critical, and the salespeople who are able to change their language will change their income immediately. And the reason that they are able to change their income immediately is because negative words like *buy, sell, sign, contract*, and others instantly give your prospect an adverse psychological reaction that actually builds objections and fight in your prospect's mind. The problem here is that as you use these negative words in your presentation, you actually create an adverse psychological reaction in your prospect's mind, and you won't know it until the end of your presentation. When you try to close the order, these negative words manifest themselves as objections. So the bottom line is that by eliminating negative words, you actually eliminate objections. Every time you say *buy* or *pay,* you may not see it, but your prospect's brain has a reaction. It turns into an objection that beats you over the head when you try to close the order.

> **This vocabulary can make an immediate and positive impact on your presentation and income.**

"Buy" vs "Invest"

The first nasty word is the word ***buy***. Never say ***buy!*** Eliminate the word ***buy*** from your vocabulary entirely. Nobody wants to ***buy*** anything. Most people have already bought too much. This is a really dirty word in sales. When you think of it from the viewpoint of your prospect, what pride is there in being a "buyer"? There is no pride in being a buyer.

The substitute for the word ***buy*** is ***invest***. When people make an investment, the nature of the word indicates that they are getting something back. Anyone can take pride in being an investor. So, remember, eliminate ***buy*** and substitute ***invest,*** because everybody wants to be an investor—nobody wants to be a buyer. Ask yourself in terms of your own self image how would you prefer to envision yourself--as an investor or a buyer? Which one would you consider a healthier self image?

"Sell" vs "Own"

Eliminate *sell* from your vocabulary! NOBODY wants to be sold; there is no pride in being sold anything. The substitute word to be used here is *own.* People don't mind owning things. They just don't want to *buy* them, and they don't want to be sold anything. People enjoy investing and owning. Additionally, from a psychological perspective, it's assumptive. It assumes that they already *own* the product.

When you use nasty words like *sell*, you will build unnecessary resistance that creates objections. And when you are walking out the door with no order in your pocket wondering what went wrong, it could be the fact that negative vocabulary set your presentation on the wrong course from the very beginning.

> **By eliminating negative words, you actually eliminate objections.**

"Sign" vs "Okay" "Authorize" or "Autograph"

We have been told all of our lives, "don't *sign* anything"—nobody wants to *sign* anything. Haven't we always been told, "Beware, don't *sign* anything"? So it is very interesting that people won't *sign* it, but they will *okay* or *autograph* it.

When you are done completing your order form, simply swing it around to your prospect, and ask him to *okay* it. It is really amazing! They won't *sign* it, but they will *okay* it! One caution here: this term may have been overused in the last ten or fifteen years. It might be wise to have an alternative, such as *authorize*. Simply hand your completed order form to the prospect, and ask him to *authorize* it. He still won't *sign* it, but he will *okay* it or *authorize* it. He or she might even offer their autograph right on your agreement.

This is not optional; it is mandatory. The word *sign* has such a negative connotation in your prospect's mind that when you say *sign,* an instant mental wall goes up. I think you can see how this vocabulary can make an immediate and positive impact on your presentation and income.

Let me give you a pop quiz: Can you think of any other negative words that you can eliminate from your vocabulary to make your sales presentation more comfortable and easier on your prospects? Read the rest of the ones on this list and then try to think of a few more. Then **eliminate** them!

"Contract" vs "Agreement"

Another very negative word in many sales vocabularies is the word *contract.* What have we heard about contracts? Beware! Be careful! "Read every word… and then have your lawyer read it. Twice." Again, let me ask you to use your mind to think of a good substitute. I can think of several: *agreement, application*, and *purchase order* come to mind. It's amazing that your prospect will not *sign* a *contract,* but he will *okay* an *agreement* or *authorize* an *application*. It's been my experience that these minor changes in vocabulary make the whole sales process less threatening to your prospect.

"Payment" vs "Investment"

Some other negative language that you can eliminate quickly include money words: *monthly* **payment***, down* **payment***, time* **payment***, price, cash price, total* **payment***.* Believe me when I say that they feel they are already making too many payments. They are already *paying* too much. Eliminate these money terms from your sales vocabulary, and again substitute *investment*. You have a "monthly *investment*," a "*quarterly investment*," an "*annual investment*." The word *"investment"* again implies that they are getting something back. And isn't that true of any salespeople selling products they believe in and use themselves? When your prospect invests in your product, he's getting something back. He's getting a return on his *investment.* And they can take pride in being an investor. What other words do we carry around that scare people?

"Deal" vs "Opportunity"

Next is *deal*—people are sick of making *deals.* They don't want to buy a *deal*. Substitute *opportunity*. Your prospect would much rather *invest* in an *opportunity* than buy a *deal*. I would definitely get more personal satisfaction offering my prospect an ***opportunity*** as opposed to selling him a *deal*.

"Pitch" vs "Presentation"

Pitch? Who gives pitches—baseball players! You are not a pitchman. That connotation goes right into the garbage disposal along with "snake oil salesman." As a professional, you give a ***presentation***, not a ***pitch***. The whole pitchman syndrome actually symbolizes the criminal element of our profession. Do you hear doctors refer to themselves as "quacks"? Or lawyers refer to themselves as "shysters"? Why should you refer to yourself as a pitchman? Take a picture in your mind's eye of the pitchman: unshaven, slovenly appearance, crooked tie with a stain on it, maybe a half pint of vodka in his jacket pocket. This is not how we represent ourselves as professionals and masters of persuasion.

> **Talk to people in "people" language.**

Trade Terminology

Last, let's talk about trade terminology. Too many salespeople take the vocabulary of our trade and force it on our prospects. For example, ***annuity***—what's an *annuity*? If your prospect doesn't know what it is, he or she doubts it. Every occupation has its own trade vocabulary. Anything that is a part of your trade vocabulary has no place in your sales presentation.

Use words that people can understand. Speak in simple "people" language. The use of negative words and too much trade terminology builds objections in your prospect's mind, and you won't even

Chapter 2

see it coming. Eliminate these words…and you will eliminate objections.

You, as a true professional, must carry yourself with dignity and integrity while providing a necessary or desirable product to a willing— even enthusiastic—prospect. Watch the words you use. Talk to people in "people" language. Relate to them on their own level, and do so projecting the correct image to your prospect so he or she can relate to you and place *trust* in you, thereby making the correct decision to invest in your product. Isn't that really the way you should think about yourself in terms of giving a great presentation?

> **Anything that is a part of your trade vocabulary has no place in your sales presentation.**

Speaking of presentations, now that we've covered the words to remove—and add—to your vocabulary, it's time to talk about how you approach your prospect and make your presentation. I'm going to give you the three steps to a dynamic presentation, and your sales numbers will never be the same again once you've understood and mastered them.

Chapter 3

The Structure of a Sales Presentation

The structure of a sales presentation is important for many reasons. The most paramount is that the sales professional understands the basic components that comprise his presentation. In almost all presentations you see—whether they're television commercials, infomercials, even print ads—you can find the structure if you analyze them. The structure of the presentation consists of the *pre-talk*, the *demonstration*, and the *close*. Let's go over each individually.

1.) The Pre-Talk

The purpose of the pre-talk, or warm-up, is to introduce your company and establish its credibility. In other words, include the length of time your company has been in business, its reputation and credibility, the quality of its products, as well as any other well-known products that your company may market.

Overall, these first few words should begin to give your prospect the feeling that he is dealing with a superior, reputable company, and he should also be gaining respect for you as you explain to him the importance of your company's reputation.

During the pre-talk you also establish your own credibility. In other words, let him know that you have been with this great company a certain period of time—possibly for years—and have studied and familiarized yourself so that you are an expert in terms of product knowledge. This gives your prospect a feeling of security as he talks with you because he knows that he is getting the best answers possible while realizing that you have accomplished certain goals as your career has progressed. The words you choose will depend entirely on your own reputation and standing in your company. If you are the number one salesman in your company, you will have a level of confidence. You will have the brightness of enthusiasm and the armor of sincerity, which will allow you to project a level of professionalism, thus giving your prospect confidence in what you say. This will actually eliminate objections.

For The New Salesperson...

It is also important here that if you are brand new with the company, take the opportunity to inform your prospect that you are new with the company in the hopes that he will give you a fair chance to earn his business—even though you may not yet be as accomplished as you would like to be in terms of knowing your product and your company's product line. This will give you a huge advantage over the old time pro, unless that old time pro has really sharpened his skills over the years. The fact that you are brand new is the most disarming thing you can say to your prospect because he thinks to himself, "This guy's brand new, he can't sell me anything."

> **If you are brand new, your prospect will actually help you get the order.**

You should always have direct access to your manager for any questions the prospect may ask that you are unable to answer. Do not stress over questions you may not be able to cover. After all, it was only after analyzing this company that you decided you could really believe in its products and wanted to represent this particular company, right? Now, believe it or not, if you are brand new, your prospect will actually help you get the order. America loves the underdog!

As I progressed in sales, I was actually reluctant to give up the benefits that being brand new gave me in terms of my customer's level of patience and almost wanting to help the new guy get a break. I did not let go of being brand new until my presentation was totally proficient—and by proficient I do not mean slick but smooth in a conversational way like one person talking to another. I guess the Zen way of explaining it would be "selling but not selling." I remember that I held on to the shield of being brand new for at least six months or until I felt that I was actually being dishonest by representing myself as new with the company.

> **You build a great presentation during the demonstration.**

Incidentally, there were times when I went out and had a trainee riding with me. Recognizing that we were dealing with a certain type of difficult customer, I told the customer that I was brand new and had to do an especially good job because my manager was watching me. And here I claim poetic license, rather than out-and-out dishonesty for trading places with my trainee because there are certain types of prospects that you will come to recognize as having certain behavior patterns. Being "new" will help you overcome the prospect's resistance.

By the end of the pre-talk, you will have put your customer at ease. You will have found some area of common ground or identification. You will be having a conversation with your customer about products. It is interesting to know that the best professionals are entirely conversational while giving their presentation—to the point where the prospect must actually think about it to remember that he is being given a sales presentation. They make it look easy—like a golf pro's swing. This is the degree of excellence that comes with experience and will allow you to be on the alert for many customer reactions, such as buying signals.

2.) The Demonstration

If you notice, every commercial on TV has some kind of a demonstration of what the product does. In many cases, you will find that the demonstration is actually the largest part of your presentation. For example, in multi-level marketing, if you are selling cosmetics, you will demonstrate the positive effects and advantages of several different familar products including skin toners, cleansers, moisturizers, eyeliners, lipsticks, etc. If you notice, when you watch a beauty product infomercial, they spend a lot of time demonstrating the different products. I think that this is probably the best example I can give you of how important a great demonstration can be when selling a line of products as opposed to a product with a single use.

> **If there is no condition and you don't get a sale, it's your fault!**

The demonstration also gives you a great opportunity to get commitments, which I will cover in Chapter 5: The Seven Steps of Successful Selling. A large part of the psychological aspect of selling is carried out during the demonstration. This includes assumptive tie downs, which we will cover in Chapter 7: Closing the Sale. An assumptive tie down is a statement that assumes the prospect is already a customer who is using the product.

As you become a true professional, you will realize the importance of your demonstration—no matter how short or how long it is. This is a part of the presentation where you become conversational. You are not selling anything. You are merely explaining to a prospect what your superior product will do and then getting him to agree. If your demonstration is not only interesting but also exciting, you will find that the level of customer participation will increase. In other words, the prospect will begin asking you questions that relate to his personal use of the product— "Will it do this?" or "Will it do that?" These questions are actually buying signals. It shows you that your prospect is visualizing himself using the product. Your ability to take advantage of these little opportunities throughout your demonstration will make your close much easier and eliminate objections.

> **In order to be a great salesperson, you must give great presentations.**

Many salespeople try to shorten, change, and even delete parts of the demonstration. From my standpoint, any salesperson who operates this way is just plain lazy and will automatically relegate himself to mediocrity. I always made my demonstration as long as I possibly could for several reasons. The longer I could hold their attention, the greater my level of control over the prospect. But most importantly, during the demonstration of any product, there are many opportunities to tell stories and to use what is called "similar situation selling"—illuminating incidences of other people's great and successful experiences while using the product.

A great lawyer once told me that winning a lawsuit is built during the depositions, and I say: you build a great presentation during the demonstration by getting the prospect to give you commitments and then confirming the commitments so that they are written in stone.

3.) The Close

Closing simply means asking for the order. You can't lose something you haven't got! Most of what I have to tell you about closing is covered in my favorite chapter, Chapter 7: Closing the Sale. Again, always remember, you cannot lose something you do not have—if you don't feel you have the sale by the time you reach the close, you haven't lost it. You must put your closing skills to work to close the order.

I can say that closing is truly an art; it's the use of psychology and the result of the foundation that you have laid all throughout your presentation. Many times when I reached the point of sale, I would remind myself over and over, "I can't lose something I haven't got!" This mantra gave me motivation to continue closing and ask for the order until I got it.

What About Conditions That Really Exist?

There is an important subject that I want to cover at this point. There is an area of sales called a *condition*. A condition is a reason for not purchasing that actually exists. When a professional salesman recognizes a condition, he packs up and leaves immediately, because in sales, time is money. If you waste your time giving a great presentation when there is no possible chance that you are going to get the order, then you lose.

What are some examples of conditions that actually exist?

    A.) No money: Your prospect has no money.
    B.) No credit: Your prospect has bad credit.
    C.) Health: Your prospect is not in physical condition to use or benefit from the product.
    D.) Age: Your prospect is too old or too young to use or benefit from the product.

These are examples of a few things that can be conditions. I am going to give you an exercise here. I want you to think of everything that can possibly be a condition. The reason for this is that if there is no condition and you don't get a sale, it's *your fault*! Believe it when I tell you that there are no such things as lousy prospects; there are only unprofessional salesmen. A professional will quickly learn to recognize a condition in order to prevent wasting a lot of time.

We have taken the time to cover the structure of a presentation briefly in this chapter, much of which I will also cover in later chapters because you need to begin understanding the framework of a sale. A sales professional understands that the proper use of a presentation is to attain a goal: writing an order, making a sale, being of service, earning a commission, and most important of all, becoming more professional. He treats his presentation the way an artist treats the building blocks of his art. Whether it's a painter who starts with a sketch, a novelist who creates the characters and plot of his story, or even a poet who creates a great couplet, I cannot emphasize strongly enough that, in order to be a great salesperson, you must give great presentations. You create a picture with words that induces your prospect to invest in your product. The result of your artistic effort is providing a service and earning money.

> **When a professional salesman recognizes a condition, he packs up and leaves immediately.**

Is a presentation all structure and rules? Absolutely not! Just like the artist I mentioned earlier, the true professional salesperson is the master of an art form. In the next chapter, I will show you how to use your creativity in your art—the lost art of sales. And after reading this, you will never have to be a starving "artist" again!

CHAPTER
4

Sales is an Art: The Introduction of Creatvity

In the first three chapters I discussed the profession of selling and merely scratched the surface of sales as a profession, the psychology and language of sales, and the basic structure of your presentation. But at this point, I feel that it is really important to understand that sales is an art. Sales is the art of creating a picture with words to entice your prospect to take money out of his pocket and invest in your product.

A painter creates a painting, goes to the art gallery, and sells the painting. An author writes a book and goes to a publisher who prints and binds the book and attempts to distribute it. And this is where the artist and the writer depend on a sales team, a gallery, or a publisher to sell their works.

A professional salesperson may have no great work to show at the end of his presentation, but he has actually transformed the thinking of another

> **Sales is the art of creating a picture with words to entice your prospect to take money out of his pocket and invest in your product.**

person—or maybe an entire group— with the creative construction of his word picture. He must sell, close, and then arrange the terms of sale immediately—and get paid for it!

Can you imagine a section in a New York art gallery that has Word Pictures written over the door or a best selling book titled *The Greatest Presentation on Earth* that is full of blank pages? This is what happens in the case of the salesperson. He uses his articulation to sell his prospect. He creates a word picture (presentation) so that when he leaves the prospect's office, living room, construction site, etc., he has a signed agreement in his pocket. Hopefully, nine out of ten of them will be good. This means that you will get a commission check or, more crassly, just plain old money.

Different Types of Salesmen

Let's take a look at several different types of world famous salespeople. First, let's look at Donald Trump, who, in his youth, was basically a rebel with a cause. Fortunately, he didn't self-destruct in a Porsche like James Dean. Donald Trump came to New York, and the first thing he did when he got to New York was to hire Roy Cohen who was, at the time, the most powerful and greatest "fixer" attorney in New York City. In fact, Roy Cohen wrote the prenuptial agreement for Donald and Ivanna, which held up in Donald's favor. So, not only was Roy an undisputed master of fixing the corruption that existed in New York City, but he was also a good lawyer. Unfortunately, due to a lifestyle behavior, he died from AIDS at the relatively young age of fifty-nine. I am definitely not passing judgment on his sexuality, merely pointing out that he was very careless.

Roy Cohen was the greatest attorney Donald Trump could have hired. He had the ability to cut through the fixes of the New York construction business, including all of its corruption, payoffs, mob influences, and so forth, like the cliché, "a hot knife through butter." This connection gave Donald Trump the ability to bypass many of the problems that plagued developers in New York City and enabled him to create a masterful success with his first big project ...and the rest is history. Trump is a flamboyant, egocentric, super-successful salesperson who built his personal brand around himself.

There are many like him, although at different levels of success. Another example is Tony Robbins who started working for me at seventeen and today conducts seminars all over the world that are attended by 100,000 people a year. His seminar in Italy last summer had seven thousand people and was simultaneously broadcast in four different languages. He is an example, like Donald Trump, of someone who has built his brand around himself.

> **We still have the opportunity in America to create an incredible standard of living...if we are willing to pay the price.**

Next is Warren Buffett, an innocuous man you would hardly notice if he passed you going to the market. My study of Warren Buffett can be summed up with his own statement, "Never buy a business whose product you don't want to use yourself." Consequently, Buffett owns See's Candies and Dairy Queen. Another example of his philosophy is to buy businesses whose products are necessary to the public. This includes Geico Insurance, who features that little green gecko. While his style of operations is completely different than Donald Trump's, both have created multi-billion dollar businesses.

Next, consider Bill Gates, who dropped out of his senior year at Harvard to start the giant Microsoft from his garage. Imagine his father's reaction when he and his partner, Paul Allen, dropped out of college and set up shop in the garage where they created a computer program that became the dominant operating system for computers around the world. Just as an aside, Bill Gates is the only entrepreneur I know of that has ever beaten the US government in an antitrust suit. All four of these great entrepreneurial, giant salespeople are prime examples of creativity, although each with his own different style.

As we progress into the next few chapters, we will study the humble beginnings of the world's highest paid profession. This statement is borne out by the fact that Bill Gates is the richest man in America, Warren Buffett is considered the second richest man in America, and while Donald Trump is not in the same league with the other two, his flamboyance and ability to build his own personal brand has probably made him more famous and more of a household name than either Bill Gates or Warren Buffett. Tony Robbins spent thirty years helping people grow so that they could make their dreams a reality.

> **I painted a mental picture of how I wanted to live, and then I moved into that picture.**

If I am going to use an example, I might as well go to the top of the heap. Very few of us who start with nothing but our own courage, integrity, persistence, and work ethic will reach the success level of these four giants. Yet we still have the opportunity in America today, which is quickly being eroded, to create an incredible standard of living…if we are willing to pay the price.

I remember the years I worked twelve hours a day, seven days a week, to master my profession. Many times my friends would taunt me with what they were going to do on the weekend or where they were going—inevitably some sort of recreational activity—and even though my lot in life was work, work, work, I loved what I was doing because it was giving me the ability to transform myself from a loser into a winner. I painted a mental picture of how I wanted to live, and then I moved into that picture.

Success like mine is harder to achieve than it used to be. The horrible recession created by men who have achieved levels of power and influence over our lives through corruption and cronyism have made your job harder than it needs to be. Many of these faceless and mostly nameless people have never made a profit at anything, not even a paper route. They have never met a payroll or been responsible to make sure that hundreds of families have a paycheck in order to eat. These same people, by making bad decisions, have brought on the worst financial crisis I have seen in all my years. Where do these people come from? Where do they go after they have stolen their millions from the public trough? I don't know. But these are definitely not the people who fuel the expansion of the greatest economy in the history of mankind.

I could go on for thousands of words describing my feelings about these worthless, negative influences and parasites sucking on the American dream, which they simultaneously criticize. But I'd much rather focus my words and energy on helping you look inside yourself to find your own acre of diamonds and fully realize your own creativity and ability to achieve no matter what size or shape you come in. I have seen creative geniuses who were five feet tall and others who were six and a half—size doesn't matter. The secret and the key here is to reach down into the God-given spirit of all humanity and dig out the most positive human attributes. Only then can we begin to focus on our core beliefs in order to achieve personal growth.

Are You Willing?

As I go into the next chapters, which, as I mentioned, are the real building blocks of selling, the amount of time, effort, and guts you are willing to invest will determine your results. One of the first things I heard from my mentor, Joe, is that you can have anything you want if you're willing to pay the price. As I paid my price over many years, I found amazing advances taking place in my life in a very short period of time. After assembling my building blocks into a foundation, I built my business and discovered creativity and energy that I never even dreamed I had. While this book is my simple attempt to communicate what I have learned, the fact that I am still taking action at nearly seventy years old by writing this book demonstrates my constant desire to grow as a person.

> **Your ability is only limited by your own thinking.**

In the next chapter you will take these building blocks and make them your own—and I do mean that you must *own* them at the deepest, psychological level, consciously and unconsciously, just like breathing. Your subconscious mind is 90% of your brain. Your conscious mind is 10% of your brain. I personally believe that God has given man, in that powerful subconscious brain, the ability to move mountains or part seas. We just have not discovered it yet for ourselves. And this uncovering, discovering, and discarding will be the genesis of the great adventure of progressing in life. The creative power that you are able to mobilize at any age or from any position on the social spectrum can be accomplished in a short period of time by understanding that, *although perfection is the ultimate goal, progress is the immediate goal.*

> **Although perfection is the ultimate goal, progress is the immediate goal.**

When we really begin to experience progress in our lives, our belief becomes stronger. That strength is, consequently, transferred into the giant powerhouse that is your subconscious mind. Many of the most successful men and women who have ever lived in America have been up and down numerous times and have failed and succeeded in business—possibly in several different businesses. They always rise again to progress toward success. Again, once you unleash this creative power, its accomplishments are truly unlimited.

The young person picking up this book, or a person of my age, can harness these universal forces to increase his ability to live well almost immediately. In fact, your ability is only limited by your own thinking. Now, unfortunately, many people have had negative influences that have affected their thinking. These negative influences have imposed crippling limitations on the ability of many people to see themselves becoming successful.

You must wipe out all negative influences! *You must truly be reborn as a clean slate, pick up a fresh set of tools* and use them persistently, creatively, and relentlessly in order to progress. Progress is the goal; none of us will ever achieve perfection. Thankfully, God has given us the ability to progress from the moment we begin to understand and use universal law and harmony until the time we move on to the next level.

As the old saying goes, inch by inch it's a cinch; yard by yard it's hard. Winners never quit; quitters never win. What the mind can conceive, the body can achieve. These idiomatic phrases are examples of the way our new thinking takes hold, both in our conscious as well as our subconscious mind.

I have fought my way through every recession since Richard Nixon who took his revenge on the State of California for repudiating him by lack of support for the Presidency of the United States in 1960 as well as the governorship of the State of California in 1964. In fact, when Nixon moved to New York to become a partner in America's oldest law firm, O'Melveny & Myers, he was quoted as saying, "California won't have Dick Nixon to kick around anymore." When he became President of the United States, it was amazing how fast the defense department contracts, which provided hundreds of thousands of jobs in California, vanished.

> **Winners never quit; quitters never win. What the mind can conceive the body can achieve.**

I was able to survive that recession from about 1969 to 1972, and I progressed. I worked through all the Arab oil embargos of the early 1970's when I had to pay gas station owners to let my salespeople show up at certain times so that they could get their tanks filled without waiting two hours in line. Whatever the problem, *I found a solution*. Whatever the hurdle, I went over it, around it, or through it. I always made progress and continually learned more and more about my profession as well as the different types of people I encountered, not only as prospects, but as people of all ages who entered the sales profession hoping to learn to live the 'American Dream' while learning to solve every problem they confronted. I made my mind up that success was mine and I fought hard for it.

Edward Harding

What Is Your Answer?

Those who did exactly what I told them to do succeeded. Those who did not practice rigorous self-honesty as well as universal law wound up taking shortcuts and indulging in other negative behaviorisms which ultimately caused them to give up. And here is the worst part: *Most of them gave up five minutes before the miracle.* I can tell you thousands of stories and expound probably for years, but the truth is that most rules of influence that were relevant then are even more relevant now.

I remember my interview with my mentor, Joe Martin. When I saw the orphaned thirty-four year-old self-made multi-millionaire and how he lived, I asked him if I could learn to do what he did. He replied, "You don't have the balls." I responded, "Give me a chance," and then he gave me his one sentence interview that I saw him give a thousand times: "Will you do exactly what I tell you to do and not think about it?" My answer was an unhesitant, "Yes." And, over the years, I saw him reject people who merely paused in answering that question. What is your answer?

By the time you finish reading this book…if you make the effort necessary to learn these tools, including handling objections and the closes, and have practiced them to the point where you can inject them into your presentation at exactly the right moment…if you can do this as conversationally as asking "Do you know what time it is?" you will find that you are consistently progressing. And believe me, this is a very good sign, because progressing in sales always translates into more money. As you wrap your brain around this simple system, which isn't taught at Harvard or Yale and yet does not apologize for itself, you will find that your experience will automatically give you solutions to problems that will baffle most people. As you gain all-important ownership of this belief system, you will find that your perceptiveness and your vision will increase miraculously. You will instantly know how to approach certain situations, and, most importantly, you will *know when to take your ego and put it in your pocket.*

There was a book that came out in 2003 called *A Course in Miracles*. A very spiritual and attractive young lady by the name of Maryanne Williamson wrote it. Some say that she took the original book and founded a cult. I say that if you absorb the steps ahead and make them second nature, you can experience your own course in miracles, and you won't be a cult member; you'll be a professional persuader. Wipe the slate clean; unleash the miraculous power within every human spirit. You will not only master the few steps that I lay out here, but you will also create the ability to go infinitely beyond what is in this simple little book.

> **Progressing in sales always translates into more money.**

With the progression of your attitude and your ego planted securely in your pocket so that you are open to learn, it is time to get you involved with the fundamental building blocks of the framework of every great presentation. How would you like to know how *the seven steps of successful selling* will make so many of your dreams come true? I thought you would, so that's why I put them in the next chapter.

Chapter 5

The Seven Steps of Successful Selling

Here comes the greatest information passed down to me by one of the most knowledgeable sales teachers of all time. I have used it all to become extremely successful. The fact is that if, at twenty-seven years old, I made a list of everything I could have dreamed of adding to my life in order to make it more perfect, I would have severely short-changed myself.

My mentor, Joe Martin, gave me the seven steps of successful selling and taught me that this is the framework upon which you build your presentation. Compare this to the frame of a beautiful Harley Davidson or the frame that is the foundation of an exotic Ferrari. More importantly, as a simile to these two metaphors, I would probably be more correct to say these are like the skeleton of the human body. The seven steps *are* the skeleton of your sales presentation.

These steps are not complicated, but they are completely essential. You must set the stage, control the situation, maintain continuity, get commitments, be enthusiastic, be sincere, and close by asking for the order. Sound like a lot to learn? Don't worry. These steps are basic…but essential. And you are becoming a professional, aren't you? Of course you are! So let's start learning by setting the stage for your presentation.

Step 1: Set the Stage

Setting the stage is simply putting the prospect in the position that is most comfortable for you to give your presentation. When you give your presentation, it takes guts to tell your prospect where you want him to sit in order for you to be able to communicate with him in the most persuasive manner.

As an example, let's take the basic in-home salesman who is putting on his presentation. You don't want Bob to be sitting in the recliner and Mary sitting in the corner of the sofa because then your head and your demonstrational information are going from side to side, like watching a tennis match. What must be done here is to tactfully ease Bob out of his recliner and ask him, even though you're intruding on his primetime television, if he could just join Mary on the sofa for a few minutes and that you will proceed as quickly as you can and get out of his hair—unless, of course, he is bald.

> **Setting the stage is simply putting the prospect in the position that is most comfortable for you to give your presentation.**

It is important to remember that tact and diplomacy are critical here, and you must remain focused on them. Then you pull a dining room chair to the center of the coffee table so that you are right across from the two of them. Never be so presumptuous as to sit in a man's chair. I can tell you that, at my stage in life, when somebody sits in my chair, it is instantly annoying. Your goal is to give a presentation that is exciting, interesting, and that literally creates a need for your product. It is important to remember not to do some unconscious little thing that immediately annoys Bob or Mary such as appearing sexist and/or focusing all your energy on Bob. Remember, in most cases, *Mary* handles the checkbook.

Here is just one example of setting the stage in the home. Make sure the TV is off! You cannot give a presentation with a television blaring in the background and somebody looking over your shoulder. Anyone who even begins to attempt this is an idiot and incapable of following the simplest of instructions, although I do understand that it can be scary to walk into someone's home and tell them that they must turn the TV off. It is still mandatory as you begin to gain control of the situation.

Today they can record whatever they were watching in primetime. It is important to understand that this could be their favorite television show; they may have been looking forward all day to sharing a bottle of wine and watching that show. So when you ask them to turn it off, you must use the greatest diplomacy. You do not tell the customer it is mandatory that he turn the TV off. If it comes to the point where it becomes so great an inconvenience that it could affect your entire presentation, you offer to reset the appointment.

> **The more presentations you give, the closer you are to the one you are going to close.**

Again remember, you are a professional. Your product could actually change their lives. Therefore, you have the right to expect their undivided attention, although out of common courtesy, it must be at their convenience. In many cases, this situation will look ideal to you—except for the fact of the television show. So reset the appointment; make sure that this lead does not go to anyone else. Most of the time your diplomacy and courtesy will be able to get them to turn off the TV, and if so, you have really begun to gain control of the situation!

I should regress here to the actual door approach. In in-home selling, you may experience some resistance at the door. Although this is not usually the case, it is still important because it is really the first act of setting your stage. In fact, some people even put signs on their door that say "No Solicitors." I love those people! When you knock on the door, don't knock like you are the DEA coming to serve a search warrant. Knock with a pleasant, unthreatening type of knock "dat-da-da-da, dat-da, dat-da." Just try wrapping that out on the table for practice. You could be the neighbor coming over to let Bob know about some important new product. Bob comes to the door, usually opening it about two feet and planting his body right in the middle. Here you create a forward momentum. Your right hand and foot move forward at the same time into his door, causing him to automatically step back, which is usually a reflex action to you stepping forward. He steps back, even if only slightly.

So now you are stepping into his living room and shaking hands with him. In the meantime, you are scanning the living room for Mary. Now I do not ever want you to think that I am being facetious in any of these examples because, as I stated earlier, the exact words are critical. Your hand and foot are creating a forward motion—just like the most beautiful golf swing you'll ever see by Tiger Woods—as you step through the threshold of his door with the goal of getting past it.

While this artful movement is taking place, you are tactfully and gracefully backing Bob out of the door and into his living room while shaking his hand and saying, "Hi, I'm [your name] with..." and name your company. "We had an appointment this evening. I believe that one of our assistants called earlier and spoke to either you or your wife to verify our appointment." In most cases, your support team should have verified the appointment. If you are selling in the home, in order to have a complete sale, you need both parties present.

When I was new, we were constantly warned about giving what is called a "one-legged pitch," which is, for instance, the situation when Mary isn't home and Bob may be having a beer and be a little bored. He doesn't mind having someone to talk to; things look good until Mary gets home and blows the whole opportunity right out of the water. And should you enter a home when the husband is absent and he comes home finding you talking with his wife? The resulting complications are obvious.

In the case where your backup team has not verified your appointment, which happens more frequently than it should, the diversionary thought process will at least give your prospect a moment's pause trying to remember whether they did or didn't call him. In the meantime, you are in the door, and it is up to you to begin your diplomacy. But always remember, if the wife is not home, you must reset the appointment after finding out when she will be home and exactly when it is convenient for them to give you a few moments of their time.

It is very important to remember when you are in the field that time is money. The more presentations you give, the closer you are to the one you are going to close and from whom you'll get the order.

I would not be so presumptuous as to equate your diplomacy with international diplomacy, but I can tell you this: your diplomacy begins here, and although you won't change world events, you will change your financial events. Remember, Bob is normally not happy to see you. You must earn his acceptance and ultimately his friendship in a very short period of time. When you introduce yourself to Mary in the same way that you did with Bob, you shake her hand, and you must remember to focus the same amount of charm on Mary as you did on Bob. In many cases, she is the decision maker. Somewhere in that living room or dining area you will spot some object—a trophy case, a bar, a painting, something that is valuable to them and of which they are obviously proud—and you immediately admire it. I cannot tell you how many times I have spent five minutes admiring a painting of Elvis on velvet. Everyone loves compliments.

In another situation, let's say maybe you are giving your presentation in an office and Bob is the purchasing agent, you have to expect interruptions such as phone calls and people popping in to ask questions. While you really cannot stop people from interrupting to ask questions, you can tactfully point out to Bob that your visit could be important to his company. Infer that it might even improve his own position, and tactfully ask if he could have all his calls held for just a few minutes.

Edward Harding

If you are telemarketing, it becomes more difficult because of the layers of insulation between you and the purchasing agent you are trying to contact. It is always better if you know the purchasing agent's name, but if you are cold-calling, you must get to the person who can make the decision to order your product. Many top telemarketing professionals with whom I have been associated and trained over the years have found that the direct approach is the best. You simply ask for the purchasing department, and from there, you ask for the manager. It is helpful if you get a receptionist to give you his or her name.

> **One of the important elements of setting the stage is creating common ground.**

Each business, depending on its size and structure, has different ways of ordering various products as well as different people who do the ordering of those products. I am sure that your company will provide excellent training. It is up to you to follow it. We must assume that their methods are successful or they would not be using them because they obviously want to stay in business.

One of the important elements of setting the stage is creating common ground. This is something that, in the course of early conversation, you find you have in common with your prospect. Here again, you must be creative. Maybe you notice a picture of his family and identify his family with yours. We are all human beings. You did not come to his home to burglarize it but rather to sell him a product that he and his family will value and use for many years. You have every reason to hold your head up high, stand tall, and be proud of your profession because you *are* a professional. If you carry yourself in this manner, your prospect will instantly recognize it and accord you the respect you deserve.

Common ground can be many things in many different areas. Maybe you both play golf. At the same time, it is critical to remember that you must also gain common ground with Mary, maybe by identifying your family with hers and your wife with her. Again, we are breaking the ice and letting our basic humanity reach out from one person to another to create what we called, in the 1960's, "a good vibe."

After you have created common ground and you have Bob and Mary in the position that best enables you to give your presentation to both of them with all the focus and personal power that you are capable of, you begin to lay the foundation for getting your order. And remember, this is *your* order. In commission sales, you get paid for what *you* produce.

This is the great thing about becoming a sales professional and being a top producer. You will never hear your boss say, "My nephew needs a job, and my sister has been on my back to put him to work, so I have to lay you off in order to hire my nephew." When you are a top producer, the nephew will have to find another job. There is an old saying that fits here: "Never put yourself in a position where a man can make a profit by getting rid of you."

I remember in my early years of selling when I made many mistakes and was fired a number of times because my individuality would often clash with a manager or general manager. As a top producer, my value was never in question because my boss understood that I made him lots of money. I hated office politics. I just wanted to become the top producer, and it had nothing to do with office politics. That achievement was strictly between me and my relationship with my prospect.

One time the general manager of a company fired me. I was the number one salesman. It so happened that the owner's office was directly across from the front door of the building with only the receptionist in between. I drove my BSA 650 motorcycle, which had a six-inch front extension—in other words, it was what you would call a chopper—right into his front door with the engine revving loud enough to rattle the windows. When I shut off the motor, walked into his office and said, "I apologize for my dramatic entrance, but I wanted to get your attention; and now that I have it, I want to point out as diplomatically as I can after driving my motorcycle into your office that you really can't afford to fire me." He looked up at me, laughed, and said, "You know something, you're right. I was wondering when you would ask for your job back, but I didn't expect a motorcycle in my front door." He told that story for many years.

> "Never put yourself in a position where a man can make a profit by getting rid of you."

This is why sales is just the greatest business. It is capitalism in the purest form. Think about it: in a capitalistic society, every person has an equal chance to do what he does best; to excel and strive for excellence; to compete; to be the best self he can possibly be. By saying "competing to be your best self," I mean that you are really competing with yourself to improve, and the result is that it enables you to compete with other salesmen with no limits in sight; it is an open-ended opportunity!

Equally important to setting the stage wherever you find your prospect is setting the stage in your mind. Setting the stage in your mind is critical and necessary and any other word I can think of to describe bringing out the winner that lives inside of you. You have to find him and bring him out. Each of us has many "selves," and when we dig into finding the best self, we must then bring it out in order to achieve our own highest and best level of accomplishment.

I used to drive down the street on my way to an appointment, and I would visualize how friendly and nice my prospect was going to be. I would visualize the immediate bonding that would take place while I was giving a great and creative presentation designed to make my product a far superior service to anything he had ever seen. If I did not believe in it, I did not sell it. If I really believed that my product was going to improve my prospect's life, then it was my job to leave with that order. This is how I set the stage in my mind. While my prospect's reaction was not always as optimistic as I visualized, I was always ready to handle any situation that took place because *the stage was set* and I had the attitude of being of service.

About thirty years ago while I was selling in the home, I went to a guy's house; he happened to be a bachelor working in construction. When he opened the front door, I was really shocked to see a seven-foot tall giant who must have weighed about four hundred pounds and whose hand wrapped around mine like I was a child. I had a pretty strong grip, but his hand could have crushed mine. This guy was so huge that I felt I was looking straight upward and talking to a cliff. When I introduced myself, he immediately informed me that he had told the person that had verified the appointment that he would give a few minutes of his time in return for his free gift. He also made it clear that he was absolutely not going to buy anything, and if I tried to sell him anything, he was going to kick my ass. I could have been a tenth degree black belt and, believe me, I would not have been able to hurt this guy with anything short of a gun.

> **Equally important to setting the stage wherever you find your prospect is setting the stage in your mind.**

Many people would have been intimidated, afraid, and wilted away in fear, but I knew that I was a professional and that I could handle any situation because my methods were mental and psychological, not physical. As long as this guy was not a psycho, I knew that I was perfectly competent to handle him mentally. And what I did was give him the greatest presentation I had probably ever given.

I love giving presentations because giving great presentations was not only my job and my meal ticket, but, most importantly, it was my *art*, which I studied and crafted to the point where I had a high level of confidence. I say confidence, not arrogance, but it is hard-earned confidence that few ever acquire simply because they are not willing to pay the price.

I took this giant man through a great, maybe even genius, presentation to the point where he made initial commitments, qualifying him to let me continue presenting our offer. In this case, my commitments were fantastic—probably triple what I needed. When I got those commitments, I started packing my sales kit. I told the prospect how much I appreciated him having the courtesy of allowing me into his home and taking his time to review our products. Now, believe me here when I tell you that I was speaking to him with the greatest sincerity because many people like this would have slammed the door in my face. I knew I had given a world-class presentation that must have at least peaked his curiosity at some level, and I was sincerely grateful that he allowed me into his home.

> **Remember, there is no situation that is a good call-back.**

When I had my kit packed, I headed for the door, and he said, "Wait, wait you haven't told me what you're selling." And I said, "No way am I going to try to sell you anything. I can definitely see that you are big enough to kick my ass as you said." And he apologized but admitted that most people who came to his home were not like me, and he really wanted to know more about our product. I still played him a little more, stating that I wanted to make sure that I was not going to get my ass kicked and needed his word on that. He grabbed my hand with his giant paw and said, "You've got my word." When I made him the offer, he immediately took it without questions or objections.

Setting the stage is the first step in creating the framework upon which you will build your entire presentation. Always take the time to do it. Never be in too big of a hurry. You will become smoother and more proficient as you practice.

Step 2: Control The Situation

If you cannot *control the situation* in the beginning, you cannot control it at the end. *If you cannot control it at the end, you cannot get the order.* This states the entire concept simply, although there is still more depth to this step. Just as setting the stage is the beginning of the framework for your presentation, it is also the beginning of gaining control because you are tactfully and diplomatically moving people around. As I mentioned during the first step of setting the stage, turning off the TV is part of gaining control of the situation.

There are many factors that can occur during your presentation, which may cause you to lose control momentarily. You must remember that it is imperative you regain that control. For example, a little kid runs in crying that his big brother is picking on him. You must allow mom or dad to restore harmony between their children...and then go back to the same position that you were in before. And here you must add something or lead back into the presentation in a way that is interesting to your prospect.

In other cases, there will be an interruption that is so severe and time-consuming that it could throw off the rhythm of your entire time in the field. Here again, you must apologize and be willing to reset the appointment at a time that is more convenient for your prospect. We must remember the old axiom, "The customer is always right," and this is really true. We are always wrong; they never are. We are taking their time, and our experience in the field demands that we move on!

> **If you cannot control the situation in the beginning, you cannot control it at the end.**

This lead may look so good because you have already overcome many of the initial barriers, gained your prospect's interest, and achieved an advantage you simply do not want to lose. There is no situation that is a good call-back, but if it has to be, then it has to be. Once again, as a professional you must make sure that you cement your budding relationship with your prospect. Be sure that it is only you who gets to come back and explain your fantastic product. By doing this, you cut off your competition and you do not have some other salesperson coming back and taking advantage of the common ground you have created. In fact, when you call dispatch to report your location, make sure the supervisor understands that this lead is to be given only to you and, even stronger, that the prospect will allow *only you* to come back into their home.

Edward Harding

As you go through your presentation and build up the customer's commitments to the point that he can, in fact, see the advantage of your product, do not be afraid to answer questions if he should interrupt you and ask one. In most cases, that question is a buying signal and demonstrates that, psychologically, the customer is envisioning himself using your product. Answer the question as positively and in as few words as possible making sure you get the prospect to commit to the fact that he understands and agrees to what you have presented up to that point. Having gained that commitment, move on through your presentation, constantly building enthusiasm and further commitments with an assumptive tie-down. A common example is, "Wouldn't you agree?"

> **You must be capable of visualizing the big picture–just as if you were a fly on the wall–in order to recognize that you are actually guiding the entire event to a successful conclusion.**

If you maintain this level of control throughout your presentation, you will find that as you enter the closing sequence, you will have established a need for your product. You will have put yourself in a position where percentages are going up in your favor. You may be interrupted by more questions, but in the majority of situations, you will not be given objections because you have not asked your prospect to buy anything yet. Your presentation has not been threatening to him in any way.

Later on when you make your offer or go for your actual close, you may get objections; we will handle the diplomacy of objections in another chapter. Here we are fully focused and concentrated on staying in control of the situation so that we can set up our prospect and put him in the best position for the close.

It is very important that your customer not think that you are setting him up at any time. If he feels that you are asking questions or making statements that are contrived and not conversational but are blatantly an effort to set him up, he will take offense and may cut you off completely. At the very least, it will be more difficult to close the sale. This is why I tell you that sales is a profession involving not only the use of psychology in handling your prospect, but also creativity and the formation and choice of your words so that you articulate a beautiful and acceptable picture with which your prospect can live.

You must be capable of visualizing the big picture—just as if you were a fly on the wall—in order to recognize that you are actually guiding the entire event to a successful conclusion. You must be capable of orchestrating the situation and recognizing any reaction, including a mere glance that indicates a negative response to your presentation. This means that you may have to go back and explain things two or three times and recommit your prospect so that he fully understands, as well as accepts, the point that you are making. You will have worked hard to get to this stage. Your level of awareness is critical, not only in maintaining control as well as any advantage you may have gained, but also in continuing with the intended flow of your presentation.

> **If you really know the presentation, you will be totally alert to every reaction your prospect gives you.**

As I mentioned earlier, you need to know your presentation like the back of your hand. If you really know the presentation, you will be totally alert to every reaction your prospect gives you and able to correct any misunderstandings that may become objections later on. Objections have their genesis in misunderstandings, a *lack of information, or language that creates fear and doubt in your customer's mind*. As a professional, you will give your presentation so that many objections that used to beat you over the head and cost you commissions will never even come up. That is why you must control your presentation in the beginning, and you must also control it all the way through to the end in order to earn that precious commission.

So, in this step, we have covered controlling the situation, and I have given you an easily understandable road map that will enable you to perform brain surgery without a knife.

Once when I was in the field with a trainee I gave a great presentation and wrote the order without an objection. The trainee remarked, "You must be a genius because you did not even get one objection." I told him that was because I had eliminated "doubt" objections during that great presentation. When you've perfected your art, this is exactly what you will do.

Step 3: Maintain The Continuity of Your Presentation

You must maintain the continuity of your presentation, meaning you give the presentation as you learned it. Do not jump all over the place. You must know your presentation as well as you know your way home through your own neighborhood on a dark night. It is not something that you have to remember; it just flows naturally as a part of your conversation.

If you are having a conversation on any other subject, such as politics, religion, the economy, the Bill of Rights—anything about which you feel deeply and that is a part of your consciousness—you know your own opinion. Your presentation is the same. It is the "thought-through" process of explaining your product so that anyone you talk to sees its merits and your viewpoint. You combine your conversational tone and your thought-through process to create the sequential close and logic of explaining it so that your prospect can accept it.

Your presentation must be in the part of your consciousness that does not require memory. This allows you the freedom to focus on the reaction you are getting from your prospect, guiding that reaction so that it flows through your mental pipeline to the point where you get the order. If you get sidetracked during your presentation by a question, as I said before, you answer the question and go right back to where you were. Continue to maintain the complete continuity of the presentation without any change.

If you do not follow this instruction, you will bounce from one sidetrack to another, and pretty soon, you will be completely off the subject at hand—your product. This cannot happen! If you allow this to happen, the result is that you lose control, and the pathway to your order has dissolved. So remember: stick to the continuity of your presentation. Do not get off the path, or you will meet the six-hundred pound gorilla who destroys your order.

> **Give the presentation as you learned it.**

I must point out that your structure continues from the beginning of the frame all the way to the back of the frame. If you weaken any part of the frame, you weaken the whole frame. The entire framework may become weakened to the point where it can destroy whatever it is that you are building. It collapses. And again, the result is that you will lose control of your sequential close.

Again, you must show some faith in your training. Those people who understand every benefit of the product far more than you will as a beginner are the ones who thought out and wrote your presentation. The people who wrote your presentation were professionals, and I am sure they tested it over and over again to make sure that it was effective.

As you go through your presentation, understand that these seven steps are the framework that you must devotedly practice. Experience will automatically tell you if you have broken the continuity or gone off track from the seven steps as a whole. If you are on a boat that is headed on a course to a definite destination and you realize that your boat has gone off course, you correct your course in order to reach the desired waypoint. In your presentation, if you find yourself drifting, you simply go back to the structure of your seven steps and correct your course. This allows you to regain control and, hopefully, reach the point down the road where you are actually depositing the commission check into your bank account.

> **Getting commitments goes on from the moment you open your mouth to the time you say goodbye.**

Maintaining continuity is the third of the seven steps, and while it is not as lengthy in terms of words, it is equally important as any other step. As an example, there were times while I was in the field realizing that I had strayed far from the continuity of my presentation and then wasted the time necessary to regain my rhythm. I put myself in jeopardy of not only losing the order at hand, but also of throwing off the tempo of my whole day. As a professional, you do not want this to happen. There will always be interruptions and distractions. That is exactly why it is so important to know your presentation so well that it does not require you to remember the words.

When you build your presentation on the framework of the *Seven Steps of Successful Selling*, you will be able to recognize your mistakes much more quickly. You will be able to recognize your mistakes and correct them rapidly, avoiding wasted time. I will continue to repeat over and over again, to the point of annoying redundancy, the importance and value of your time. You did not come to stand in line, but you must exhibit diplomacy and courtesy if there is an interruption that throws you off so badly that it interferes with your entire days' sense of rhythm; time to reset.

You always have the option of looking at your watch and saying, "You know, I have an appointment, and I didn't mean to get so far off track, but I would certainly appreciate it if you would allow me the professional courtesy of resetting this appointment and coming back to see you as my first appointment tomorrow." This is a way to maintain not only the continuity of your presentation, but also your entire day. Many times you will be forced to make a judgment call. Is your prospect so receptive to your presentation that you feel it is worth the risk? Then go ahead; take the extra time you need to get that order you feel is in the bag. If you are dealing with the other type of prospect where you feel the order is going to require more work and a much more detailed explanation, then you can decide to reset the appointment to provide more time and fewer interruptions. In fact, your prospect may tell you that if you come back at a certain time, he would be able to devote the undisturbed time you need.

While the continuity step requires fewer words than some of the other seven steps, it does not diminish the importance of *maintaining* this continuity. Skipping all over the place when the prospect interrupts with a question on a subject that you will cover later in your presentation should not throw you off kilter. You simply say, "If you would be patient with me, I'm sure I'll cover that later in my presentation." Do not give up your continuity! Do not put yourself in a position of walking out, scratching your head, and saying, "What did I do wrong here?" Make these steps your rules of influence, and stick to them throughout your presentation. I have trained thousands of men and women who have done what I suggest here, and they have become extremely successful; many times catapulting themselves into seven-figure incomes.

> **A commitment is any question that makes your prospect agree with you and say yes to a tie-down question.**

Step 4: Get Commitments

A commitment is any question that makes your prospect agree with you and say yes to a tie-down question; get as many as you can. Build strength and power into your presentation by making your prospect agree with you over and over and over again. In other words, if, during the course of your presentation, the prospect says yes to you and agrees with you at least a hundred times that your product has value, he is now psychologically in the habit of agreeing with you. And, obviously, this makes it much harder for him to disagree at the end.

If I said to you that it is really important you do whatever it takes to help your children get good grades in school—even if it involves sacrificing in order to spend extra money to hire a tutor—wouldn't you agree? Wouldn't you say that these newly achieved goals enable your children to tackle that test with their heads high and with the confidence that they have the knowledge to answer the questions? Wouldn't you agree with me that this is important? Here you have an example of a commitment, which I purposely related to your personal life. If I were the salesperson, I might be selling the somewhat expensive services of one of those many learning/tutorial centers across the country. And that commitment question may motivate you to make the sacrifice to spend the extra money to help your children get better grades. Do you see what I mean?

When you ask your commitment question, such as, "Wouldn't it be important to make the sacrifice and investment to ensure that your child walks into his classroom with his head held high, bursting with confidence because he knows the subject matter?" What do you think he will say? I doubt he would rather have his child face the fear of failure due to lack of knowledge as well as the negative attitude and disdain he will feel from his teacher. "Do you see the point of what I'm saying? Do you follow me? Wouldn't you agree that this is critical to your child's development?" I have just given you three assumptive tie downs. These would make your prospect say yes and agree with you over and over again, ultimately coming to the point of feeling very guilty if he does not make sure his child has the best education in order to develop as a human being. How can he refuse without admitting he doesn't love his kids?

- Do you see what I mean?
- Wouldn't you agree?
- Do you get the point?
- Do you follow me?
- Isn't it so?

These are some tie downs to your commitment questions that build your order throughout your presentation. In fact, these are *mini closes*. In other words, you are asking little closing questions all throughout your presentation so that your prospect agrees with you, as I said, at least a hundred times.

The psychological tactic you are using here is presenting a point during your presentation and then following it with an assumptive tie-down. Why? Because it's true! And if you do not act as a professional and reach through to get inside your prospect's consciousness so that he can see the value of what you are saying, you are doing him a disservice that can have a significant influence on his life. In this example, you put your prospect in the position where he is asking himself whether he loves his child enough to do the right thing. What follows? An ego conclusion. Getting these commitments goes on from the moment you open your mouth to the time you say goodbye and get in your car. It is a process that never stops, and it is really so simple.

> **By the end of your presentation, you must psychologically posture yourself to *expect* that order.**

I will give you another example. Nine times out of ten, if you look at your prospect and say anything resembling the truth, and nod your head while you are saying it, he will start nodding his head with you. So, here you have him nodding his head "yes," and you haven't even asked for a tie down.

Think about the power you can pull from inside yourself and muster up in order to present a true belief. It's kind of funny. While I was selling, there were times when I did not get the order. I felt that if I did not get the order because of my presentation, I would not leave unless there was blood on the carpet. In fact, many times after I did my best—yet failed to get the order because one party admitted he lied to me or reneged on his commitment—I wanted to make sure that the next time he was put in the same position, he would make the right decision.

> **I believe that the sales professional, after giving a great presentation, is entitled to get the order.**

Maybe it's funny, and maybe it seems harsh, but if I did not get the order when I left the house, the husband and wife would be attacking each other like two pit bulls. I am not suggesting that you take satisfaction from someone's personal discomfort because they lied to you during your presentation or reneged on their major commitment. But I did take some satisfaction because I believed that what I was selling would improve their lives or I would not be selling it.

During my presentation, *I usually received at least one hundred commitments and tie downs throughout the process*. This should have made it impossible for them to say no at the end unless a true condition existed. As you will remember, I spoke about conditions earlier. If a condition exists, you cannot get a sale no matter how good your presentation. It is up to you to determine this *early* in your presentation, and hit the road if there is a condition! Do not be so disengaged that you only find out at the end that your prospect has a condition. You should have discovered it earlier, not at the time you expect to be writing an order. From my own personal viewpoint, when I gave a great presentation I expected to get the order. Of course there are always exceptions to the rule.

So, in step number four, **Getting Commitments**, I cannot emphasize strongly enough the importance that these commitment questions be consistently built into every presentation and "nailed" with an assumptive tie-down. If you build the opportunity you are trying to sell with the psychological strength of super glue, believe me, you have a right to expect your order at the end. You have done your job well and now expect to reap the reward.

It does not make any difference whether you are selling airplanes, boats, cars, language tapes, household appliances, cosmetics, beauty aids, vacuum cleaners, encyclopedias, education, food, medicine, clothing, or any of the other millions of products that exist in our world today. By the end of your presentation, you must psychologically posture yourself to *expect* that order. If you do not get it, you are entitled to know the reason why. Now, I am not talking about arguing with your prospects. I am talking about asking questions that lead them to a certain conclusion. If they do not reach that conclusion, then it is not logical. And as a professional, I promise you, I will find out why. In Chapter Seven I will teach you the *Lost Sale Close*.

Here again, I am not trying to build an attitude of hostility, but I am trying to help you understand that if you give your presentation correctly, you have the right to get that order—or to know why you did not get the order. Unless a real condition exists, there are no stupid prospects—there are only lazy, unqualified, unprofessional salespeople who fail to practice or learn the basic principles of their profession. This offends me to the point that in every training session I conduct, I attempt to stomp out the mealy-mouth attitude of not standing up for yourself after you have given a great presentation and the prospect has agreed with you continuously for a duration that could be from an hour to all day. You *must* do your job properly and get that order—*now,* today!

I do not care what the product is. If your principles are sound and you do not get the order now, you will not get it later. I repeat, if for some reason you did *not* get the order, do not leave that sales situation without a complete understanding of where you failed, even if it requires forcing your prospect to admit that he lied to you. I am not trying to be overly harsh, but I believe that the sales professional, after giving a great presentation, is entitled to get the order—or to leave blood on the floor, because I will certainly never be back there again. (I want to clarify that if you are in a situation where you are selling fifty jumbo jets, the time period may be a month, but the principles are the same.) If you had been a professional all the way through, you need to know the reason why you did not get that commission so that you can be sure never to make the same mistake again.

So, here we have the importance of commitments. I am sure many of you have seen the little dolls that people put on the dashboard of their car where the head bobs up and down. That is the same action you want from your prospect; you want that head bobbing up and down all the time.

Almost every presentation has a major commitment. It could be related to the use of the product or need for the product or even understanding the value of the product in planning for one's retirement. But it is, in fact, the commitment question that is really very critical. Unless you get that commitment, pack it all up and leave. Why? Because you are a professional, not a doormat; you did not come to put on a free show. Unless your prospect answers "yes," hit the bricks and get on to the next one because that person just became another number in what is actually a numbers game. I must emphasize this very strongly.

On the other hand, perhaps this is the point where you determine that there is actually a condition that will prevent you from getting your sale. Again, if you do not get an affirmative answer to that commitment question, get on your way to the next appointment. Strangely, though, you may notice that when people see you leaving in a hurry and not wasting your time, they wonder why you are not hanging around to beg them for the order. They do not know it, but this is because you are not a beggar, you are a professional, and time is money. They may actually ask you why you are leaving so soon. At this point you can courteously and tactfully explain to them that they have just demonstrated that they do not qualify for your product or your time in presenting it to them. This is where a negative close could be used effectively.

I cannot tell you how many times, after failing to get affirmative answers to key commitment questions, people were surprised when I actually got up and left. I explained to them—with a smile on my face, a sparkle in my eye, and courtesy in my tone of voice—that I did not come here to push them or pressure them into investing in something that would not be of value to them. My purpose is to agree with them, assist them, and be of service. I explained that, in this situation, it did not seem that I would be able to meet those expectations. At that point they may try to re-explain themselves. Like I said, often when they saw that I was willing to get up and walk out the door, their whole attitude changed, and *the resistance that was causing me to fail to get that key commitment melted away.*

I then apologized for being so abrupt and told them that I was sure they could understand that this is how I made my living and supported my family. It is not in anyone's best interest—mine or theirs—to waste anyone's time. You will see this come up over and over again as I deal with the chapters *Handling Objections* and *Closing the Sale*.

It is also so important that I point out to you that when you ask the commitment question, you must *shut up*. You do not speak again until your prospects respond. There may be dead silence. You will be amazed at how many times in your presentation your silence exerts the greatest pressure you could possibly command. Most people cannot stand ten seconds of silence. Be sure that when you ask the commitment question—which is actually a trial close—you shut up until they respond. Then proceed as I indicated above. Overcoming that initial resistance will, most likely, reverse the situation. You may then continue with the remainder of your presentation, including every commitment you can possibly think of, and you will find that it will flow in perfect harmony. The ensuing positive conversation will lead to the direct deposit of a commission check.

> **In your presentation, your silence exerts the greatest pressure you could possibly command.**

Step 5: Be Enthusiastic

Here is where we begin the magical mystery tour of selling while bringing out the spiritual nature of the sales process. **You must be** *very enthusiastic in your presentation.* The word *enthusiasm* comes from the Greek root *entheos; en* meaning "in;" *theos* meaning "God." I refer to the spiritual steps of selling because when you are enthusiastic, you are inspired. You exhibit a strong excitement or a special belief that empowers your presentation with the greatest dynamism in the universe. For agnostics or atheists, we can translate "God" to "energy." In other words, you are tapping into the greatest energy source in the universe. It flows through you to your prospect, and following the law of Karma, ultimately comes back to you.

> **The communication of strong excitement and inspired feelings transcends the human ego.**

Understanding that these universal laws are as powerful as the law of gravity is critical. They are the universal principles upon which every civilized thought process is founded. More simply put, *you get back what you put out*. If you are enthusiastic with your prospect, he or she will react to you and be more enthusiastic. Again, enthusiastically tap into the universal power of your great core belief system, and your prospect will automatically feel your enthusiasm and react likewise. *The communication of strong excitement and inspired feelings transcends the human ego.*

It is vitally important for you to understand the significance of aligning yourself with the greatest of all powers, the universal principle or universal law. The laws of nature create situations that instantly become much more harmonious—and isn't harmony what we are trying to accomplish during our sales presentation? We achieve basic mental alignment or harmony with our prospects throughout our presentation. Reflectively, they pick up your energy and return it back to you. I repeat this about three or four times because this spiritual step of selling is highly important. This magical mystery tour creates enthusiasm, and enthusiasm creates magic in selling. While I may have oversimplified the process, the simple fact is that your prospect really feels your enthusiasm, and this can make all the difference in the world!

I know people who jump out of bed in the morning and yell, "Boy, am I enthusiastic!" I know people who also get out of bed and ask that they be able to experience God's presence in their life today. Either of these actions will assist you in setting the stage in your mind; this is necessary in order to go out and give your best presentation.

Many people wake up some days and they don't feel enthusiastic, they don't feel hope, and they don't feel that their soul is in touch with universal harmony. To those people, I say, "Fake it 'til you make it." In this case, you will be one of those people who jump out of bed and yell, "Boy, am I enthusiastic," until you start to laugh at yourself because you are actually beginning to feel it. There is no way to quantify the importance of real enthusiasm as a part of the great presentation except to say that without it you are dead in the water. Your presentation will be bland, ineffective, and mediocre—at best.

> **Sincerity is defined as earnestness, and your presentation must have both.**

Step 6: Be Sincere

Sincerity is defined as earnestness, and your presentation must have both. An earnest and sincere feeling champions the quality of being open and truthful, not deceitful or hypocritical. Your sincerity will inspire belief, which, in turn, will cause your audience to believe what you say and to feel the authenticity of what you are communicating.

For example, if I were to say to you, "Can you loan me one hundred dollars?" If you perceive me as a sincere person, you figure that I will pay you back. Therefore, you are willing to risk loaning me the hundred dollars. Here we can analogize sincerity as another spiritual step in selling and realize the believable significance of its power. Sincerity transcends the human ego in communication and creates the belief system necessary to invest yourself in a product. When you project this to your prospect, he will trust and believe you.

I do not want to sound like a "bible thumper," but I must emphasize the importance of the spiritual side of selling. It is in these two steps that you can find yourself tapping into the vast and unlimited power of natural law and applying it to your sales presentation. Our unlimited power comes from within and the practice and understanding of natural law. Applying that understanding energizes and produces a *great* presentation. This identifies the real professional and enables him to not only succeed in the instant selling opportunity but also to inspire others throughout his career.

> **Our unlimited power comes from within.**

The return gift is to progress to the next level where the use of this unlimited energy empowers you to build a team, and as a sales manager, to earn the holy grail of sales, which are the overrides. At this point you will find that you may have many people whose production earns you income. If you live in New York, you may be earning money while you are sound asleep as your teammates are busy selling on the West Coast. Never forget that your spirituality can help you achieve your dreams and open the door to unlimited success.

During my career as a sales manager, I had over five hundred people under my leadership. I taught them the inspiration of enthusiasm and sincerity; they worked harder, longer, and more effectively than they ever dreamed possible, all because of the belief system they acquired while becoming a professional in the world's highest paid occupation. As they progressed through each step, they saw the proof and realized the power of the endeavor. These wonderful men and women created their own reality and continued moving forward to the next level.

This is a high ideal. I want to remind you that you cannot set for yourself the impossible goal of perfection, but as your experience progresses, you will find yourself proving your own belief system. There will be times when progress seems to be coming slowly. *We must remember that the goal is progress in any amount,* whether we achieve it an inch at a time or whether we move rapidly through the challenges that we will ultimately confront. Every inch of progress gives us proof, and in some situations in life, your actual survival will depend on that realization. I hope that I have not over-simplified or over-intellectualized these last two steps. Although they are critical factors throughout life, the bottom line is simply remembering that you get back what you put out.

Step 7: Close — Ask For The Order

Closing means asking for the order and remembering that you cannot lose something that you don't have. In other words, you cannot lose an order if you do not ask for it, and if you do not ask for it, you will never get it.

When I was younger and striving with every fiber of my being to become a professional, I found myself in closing situations. As I consciously built my presentation around the *Seven Steps of Successful Selling*, I remember saying to myself, "You can't lose something you haven't got; you can't lose something you haven't got." That simple mantra gave me the courage to ask for the order. Increasingly I learned to get the order, but as I attempted to make crystal clear earlier, if I did not get the order, I made sure I knew why so that I would not make the same mistake again.

> **You cannot lose something that you don't have.**

As you go out and build your presentation using the *Seven Steps of Successful Selling* as a framework, you will find yourself continually checking to make sure you have completed each step in order to achieve the greatest presentation. In the beginning, your efforts may seem clumsy, but continued practice will never fail to give you the advantage of improving. And the realization that even though your prospect may have met many salespeople, *he hasn't met **you**.*

Edward Harding

As you grow and build yourself step-by-step, you transform into the person you really want to be—the hero in your own life. In 1963, listening to Bob Dylan's song, "It's Alright, Ma," with his lyrics, "I ain't got nothing to live up to," I understood exactly how he felt because I felt the same way. If *you* feel the same way, then you have a *great* choice to make: you can stay that way, or you can build *yourself* into the person *you* want to be—the one you can look up to.

> **Even though your prospect may have met many salespeople, he hasn't met you.**

So there you have them—the seven steps to successful selling. You must set the stage, control the situation, maintain continuity, get commitments, be enthusiastic, be sincere, and close by asking for the order. If you stick to this framework, you will be amazed how your numbers increase. However, you probably already know that things rarely go according to plan. People have real conditions, and you must be willing to use your time wisely by walking away.

But what about objections? These are not conditions; they are illegitimate barriers the prospect puts up to resist your sale. You can follow all seven steps...and still encounter them. How do you overcome them? I am glad you asked, because that is why I wrote the next chapter. Get ready to learn how to handle objections!

Chapter 6

Handling Objections

I want to make it clear that while all chapters are important, this is one of the most essential chapters of this book. The information is critical. You must learn it and *put it into action* immediately to have any benefit in your life, and improving your life is the reason I wrote this book…and you are reading it.

I sense that we are losing something as human beings. We are losing something we cannot afford to lose, no matter what our ethnicity, economic situation, color, or station in life. The guidance set forth in this chapter gave me the opportunity, as I have previously stated, to make a full 180-degree change in my life. It enabled me to transform myself, with Gods' grace, from a bum into the person I really wanted to be—and even the hero of my own life.

> **Handling objections requires diplomacy.**

When I look in the mirror, I look deep into my own soul. I like what I see, although I, like every other human being, have faced problems and challenges. Today the inside of my head is the place where I really want to live. My motive here is to share this information with anyone who wants to make a change, so get ready to improve your life!

Handling Objections Requires Diplomacy

Diplomats, whether at the UN or the State Department, practice just that: diplomacy. My sales training with Joe Martin was with the greatest sales trainer of all time. I have studied many experts, but he is the one who introduced me to J. Douglas Edwards, a man whose methods *undeniably work*. And I listened and accepted that instruction without reservation because, as I said earlier, I had the humility to be taught. But most importantly, Doug Edwards' strategies are simple and can be adapted to any presentation. They make sense…good, common sense.

When I began to listen to Mr. Edwards, I knew that what he was teaching was exactly what I needed to learn. Much of what I cover in this chapter are methods I learned from J. Douglas Edwards. I am not plagiarizing him, but I am attempting to communicate to you the same things that I learned, with my own observations, lessons, and thoughts on why he is so effective and in both his words and my own.

> **As I said before, the magic word is *action*.**

You must learn this material…and then put it into action. As I said, *the magic word is action*, and you must not give up when you find that your first attempts are fumbling and ineffective. I promise you, if you practice these methods, master them, and then put them into action—making them conversational just like talking to your neighbor—your income will increase *immediately*. You will believe more than ever that the steps I am giving you work as you see your results and income increase. You will soon find yourself with a natural belief system that controls how you think and feel about your profession, the way you practice your master sales persuader role and these rules of influence.

In chapter two, I talked about the *language of selling*. It is not my intent to be redundant, but I must make it crystal clear that redundancy in sales is sometimes necessary – although you don't want to become boring! You may recall watching television commercials that tell you to call a phone number, and call it now; that phone number will appear 5-10 times. This redundancy becomes the closing sequence of the television commercial. They may even tell you, "You have nothing to lose, so call now!" Redundancy is also important in the diplomacy of handling objections.

All salesmen must rid their vocabulary of language that builds objections. This must be foremost in mind the minute you begin to speak. The *nasty* words must not come out of your mouth, or they will begin building objections and fight in your prospect's mind.

Let's quickly recap these *nasty* words to avoid: buy, sell, sold, contract, sign, payment, down-payment, time payment, price, monthly payment. I repeat these words hoping that you will understand that nobody wants to hear them. When they come out of your mouth, you instantly build a wall or doubt that creates an objection. Everyone has already bought too much. Nobody wants to be sold. As I listen to people trying to persuade me to purchase their product today, I hear and see an appalling lack of professionalism on the part of professional persuaders trying to convince me to purchase their product. I listen to people selling products today—and I am purposely using this nasty word "sell" because that is what they are doing whether in direct marketing or telemarketing—and I can instantly tell they are not at all professionals. Telemarketers call me on the phone, and rarely do I hear a professional presentation because the *nasty* words they use immediately build a wall in my mind. I believe in the natural law that if I feel this way, other people must feel the same. Similarly, nobody wants to be sold anything, yet salesmen are constantly bombarding their prospects with these words: when I *sell* you, when you *buy*, the best *price*. When a salesman is lacking the proper training or has become too lazy to use the correct vocabulary he puts up a wall with his prospective customer. Then he wonders why he gets resistance…

> **People do not like to buy things, but they do not mind owning them.**

Edward Harding

You will recall that the substitute for these words are *own, invest, authorize,* and *okay*. People do not like to buy things, but they do not mind owning them. In addition, owning is assumptive. Remove from your vocabulary the words buy, sell, sold; substitute *own*. Put yourself in the prospect's position. When the salesman swings a contract around and asks you to sign it, I know that you feel you must read every word or you will get trapped, because we have all been told since childhood to never sign anything—watch out, read it twice, then doubt it. And it's true! Many companies have rooms full of lawyers inserting trick clauses and legal jargon into their contracts. We are told that even when we read it, we must doubt it.

I have, in the process of doing business, negotiated many contracts that my wife and I had to go over, edit, and rewrite…up to fifteen times, taking maybe a hundred hours of work! Believe me, even though most people are not as diligent as we are—and by the way, we do not have our own room full of lawyers, we just have our own common sense to protect ourselves—you must not be afraid to say, "I don't understand what this means; please explain it to me." When we have reviewed the language of each clause, we eventually find that we have something we can agree upon, and we are perfectly willing to authorize or okay it. When somebody sends us a contract and tells us to *sign* it, a red flag goes up automatically.

When you have made an agreement with your prospects and decided on the terms, you simply hand it to them with your pen and ask them to *okay* it, or *authorize* your agreement or purchase order. People are perfectly willing to *authorize* something they agreed to and to *okay* something that they have already discussed and decided upon.

I apologize again for the redundancy, but the language here is critical, and again, these are key points of diplomacy. Other undiplomatic areas of language are the money terms we covered: *pay, price, payment, down payment, monthly payment, semi-annual payment, cash price*. The basic problem with these words is that people are already making too many payments. If you never heard anybody say that to you, then you can skip to the next page, but I doubt that there are any professional persuaders who have not learned this lesson…and learned it well.

Remember, the substitute we have for these terms is that we *invest*. I am an investor. I like to *invest* in things because I feel that, if I make a great investment, I will get a great return. *Prospects do not mind being investors* or having an original investment, a quarterly investment, an annual investment, a total investment. When they *invest*, they take pride in the thought of receiving a return.

Check your presentation for language and any words that might put your prospect "on guard." Once you lose the comfort level with your prospect as we discussed previously, it is difficult—if not impossible—to get it back. If you traded places and listened to yourself, you would not buy it either.

As I said, I take pride in being an investor, and along the way I talk to people individually and in groups about investing. Recently I spoke at Cal State Fullerton, which I have done annually for a few years—I love it. I wish I could talk to more of the young people who are going to make the *real* changes of the future. After I finish speaking, I am often surrounded by a group of 18-22 year-old people who want to ask me questions. Sometimes I encounter negative attitudes, just as you see all over the world when people say terrible things about American business, whether it's hedge funds, automobiles, or Wall Street. Once I actually found myself getting angry with a young man who was about 6'3" and weighed about three-hundred pounds. I won't give you his name, but believe me, I remember it, and I actually reached the point where I put my finger in his chest and asked him to name one thing in the world that had not been invented in America. He thought and he thought, and this well-educated genius could not come up with an answer. A few world-changing things have not been

> **It is up to each one of us to know our core beliefs and to shine the light of truth into every situation.**

invented in America, but they are the exception, not the rule. But if you think about it, you will find that America has earned its place in the business world. And yes, there are people out there with excessive greed; they are screwing things up! That is why it is up to each one of us to know our core beliefs and to shine the light of truth into every situation in which we find ourselves.

As I already pointed out, another area of distasteful verbiage is in using trade terms. When I asked this same young man what he wanted to be when he went into business, he replied that he wanted to be a business advisor to people making investments that would affect the rest of their lives. I asked him what a hedge fund was, and he launched into a dissertation about investments and derivatives that seemed like they were in a foreign tongue. I told him that I did not understand what he was saying, that he might as well have been speaking another language, and that if he wanted to advise people on how to invest, he would definitely have to get rid of those trade terms and talk in "people language."

> **Clean up your language and the objections beating you to death will automatically disappear.**

I remember while listening to J. Douglas Edwards that he talked about radio salesmen trying to sell *spots*, and that he had a dog and on his carpet he had spots. He didn't want to buy any more of those. He also said that a spot was something on his shirt, and he had to take it to the cleaners to get it out. Yet a salesperson wanted him to pay money for a spot. The world has changed greatly since the days of Doug Edwards. The motivators of that era referred to computers as electronic brains; now we have them in our telephones. The point is to eliminate trade terms from your presentation and talk to people in "people language." Always check yourself for any terms that scare people. Use words people understand because you are in the business of *communicating* with *people*. You must make them understand the words you speak so that they can make the decision you want them to make and purchase your product.

Another bad word is *deal*. People do not want to make *deals*. The word automatically makes me feel like something is corrupt which, I would say is a bad connotation. The substitute word is *opportunity*. I love to sell opportunities. I believe that any product in which I get involved offers people the opportunity to make their lives better.

And last but not least, as I said in the second chapter, lose the word *pitch*. We are not pitchmen; we are not peddlers. We do not give pitches; we give *presentations*. We are the people who make every product in the world move, and, without us, distribution of the necessities of life would cease.

> **Your job is to prove your prospect right–so that he wants to purchase your product.**

You need to choose the words you say to make sure that they do not cause doubt, fear, confusion, or a lack of information. Using nasty language results in today's professional persuader having to work harder at his diplomacy in order to handle objections rather than eliminating them in the beginning. Clean up your language, and many times you will find that the objections that are beating you to death will automatically disappear.

Nothing Like A Warm Body...

Before we get into the principles of diplomatically dealing with objections, I want to take a moment to describe why this is so important. In today's world, we deal with many vendors. After we go through a maze of computer questions where it asks us for our name, our account number, our birthday, our social security number, our driver's license number, and our secret password, we still don't get a warm body to deal with. We all know the frustration this creates.

If we do get a warm body to talk to after waiting and wasting our time, maybe ten or fifteen minutes, the tops of our heads are about to blow off. We usually get some snotty customer abuse agent whose primary goal seems to be to get you off the phone as fast as he or she can. It is very sad that we have lost diplomacy in handling objections or problems that come up in the sale of every product. We must get our training level back to the point where we diffuse our prospect's anxiety, thereby reducing the level of anger. Frankly, I have had times where my blood was boiling and the top of my head was about to come right off; I just hang up. These companies certainly lost the possibility of up-selling or suggesting additional products to me.

A Few Timeless Diplomatic Principles

In the diplomacy of handling objections, the language, the time—the decade, even the century—may change, but certain principles remain the same.

The first principle is not to argue; do not *ever* fight with your prospect. Doug Edwards referred to an example of this as happening in the boxing ring. This thought stayed with me over the years because when I was young, I did some amateur boxing. Today I still work with a speed bag just to keep my reactions sharp. When you get into the boxing ring, you do not want to stick your jaw out and walk into a punch. You are most likely to get knocked out. The way you avoid a punch is to bob, weave, block, and roll with the punch. You do not *ever* fight your prospect. In sales, you *do not* argue with your prospect.

> **Do not *ever* fight with your prospect.**

I have known many people who are very articulate powerful speakers and great debaters. The idea is not to win the debate or win the argument; the idea is to persuade the prospect to alter his thought process so he can purchase your product. I cannot tell you how important this is: you never fight, you never argue.

I recently got an acquaintance of mine a job. He is forty-two years old and could not make a dime. The job was with a very successful friend of mine in the telemarketing business. When I called for a report, my friend told me that his new employee was a great debater, and, in fact, he could win every debate. The problem was that he just was not selling anything; he was too busy keeping track of his debating strategies. I had to have a meeting with my acquaintance and teach him to take that ego and put it in his pocket. When a salesman gets an objection from a prospect, he can choose to fight him endlessly. Even if the prospect wins the argument and proves that the salesman was wrong, that prospect is still going to be upset. Your job is to prove your prospect *right*—so that he wants to purchase your product.

Remember what we have said about *conditions*—they are reasons for not buying which *truly exist*. When you recognize a condition, you must move on—you don't argue, you *move on*. Believe me, your employer does not want you to be out there selling bad *deals*—and again, I purposely used the word "deal" here because of the negative impact. Your employer does not want you cutting corners and bringing in deals that you have misrepresented, which inevitably become a problem.

When you run into a condition, it is important to make sure that you explore it to ascertain if it is real. To paraphrase Doug Edwards, if your prospect says that he is too old, too old for what? Is he too old for your product or too old for girls? There may be a vast difference in understanding the subject, so make sure you explore the condition and its validity.

> **The greatest salespeople in the world look for objections and mark them as areas of interest.**

Remember, if no condition exists and they do not invest in your product, *your presentation was not good enough.* "There are no lousy prospects; there are only lousy salesmen. If he qualifies and a condition does not exist and he does not buy, you eat it, it's your fault."

As we have said, objections and conditions are two very different things. What creates an objection? An objection is normally caused by a lack of information, a misunderstanding, or failure on the part of the professional persuader to cover all the information during that great presentation. An objection can be an illusion; it can be fear; it can be a natural resistance that your prospect gives to everybody.

The greatest salespeople in the world look for objections. *They seek them out* because they know that they have the ammunition to overcome any objection. When I was selling in the home thirty-five years ago, I found that people agreed with me and went right along with me. When I got to my basic order form, which was a credit application, I learned that they had been laid off or had another condition. When I went back that night to critique my presentations with my sales manager, he ripped my head off! "You mean to say you wasted two hours of your precious time to find out that somebody was laid off when you could have handled it with a simple question like, 'How did it go at work today?' way back in the beginning?" This prospect knew he could not buy. I was not smart enough to qualify this prospect for conditions that may truly exist, so the prospect just enjoyed a little free show and robbed me of my time in the field. And believe me, *time is money*. I am sure you will find this out after wasting hours and hours giving presentations to possibly well intentioned people who are merely curious to see what is out there in the market place. These curiosity seekers will waste your time looking for ideas that they may find beneficial to themselves.

> **If it is a valid objection, what will happen? He will ask it again.**

When I say that the smart salesman looks for objections, I mean that he identifies objections because this is where the professional determines what his prospect is interested in buying. It *announces* the area of his interest and what is important to him. If it were not important, he would not bring it up in the first place. The smart salesperson looks for objections. He *marks them* and realizes that this is an area of interest that is going to cause this prospect to buy. In studying many teachers, I have found that Doug Edwards' methods were the most simple, most direct, and easiest to *put into action*. Let us look at his basic five-point plan for handling an objection.

Step 1: Bypass It!

"The first time you hear the objection, bypass it—always. Never answer it." Why would we bypass an objection and not jump on it? Because this is what *everyone else* does. They jump on the objection, and right away it is argumentative and becomes solidified in the prospect's mind. We know that people have a series of standard objections that they give to everyone.

The first time you actually hear an objection from your prospect, you bypass it and move on through your presentation. Your choice of words could be, "Yes, but…" But this is blunt and harsh. The proper way to respond is, "Yes, sir, I can see why you would feel that way. By the way…" and you move on. Always acknowledge your prospect; let him know that you understand how he feels. Cushion your response with, "By the way…" and move right on through your presentation. If you do this, you will find that a large percentage of objections that arise in every presentation will *eliminate themselves*. You bypass it, and he does not bring it up again—because it was not valid in the first place. If it is a valid objection, what will happen? He will ask it again. Now you have a valid objection to handle.

Step 2: Shut Up And Listen!

The debaters out there today hear three words and they think they know what their prospect is going to say. They interrupt their prospect mid-sentence—which makes the prospect angry—answering what they think he is going to ask. Well, guess what? Even if you guessed right, your prospect is going to be irritated. There is this little thing called respect: *hear your prospect out, listen to him*. I hope he is listening to you. If you do not listen to him, you are simply a fool and will remain an order taker.

Step 3: Question It!

After you have heard your prospect out, question the objection. This is where you put your ego in your pocket, trade places with your prospect, and respond to his concern. Simply say, "Just so that I don't get confused, sir, [you're the dummy, he never is] what brought that particular issue to mind at this point?" Again, *listen*, because here is where he is making his decision. When you question the objection and he answers or explains it, it may sound ridiculous even to him; but it could also bring out a hidden objection. You only find this out if you question it.

Step 4: Answer It.

After you have questioned it, answer the objection fully, leaving no stone unturned regarding any area of relevant information. Once you have answered the objection fully, usually nodding your head up and down, go to step five.

Step 5: Confirm The Answer.

Your next line is, "Now, that settles that, doesn't it, sir?" When you have reached a secure level of sincerity, confirm the answer and say, "Now sir, in all sincerity, I have completely clarified this question, haven't I?" If you have confirmed the answer to his satisfaction, the objection will go away, and it will not come up again. You will not find yourself in that impossible situation of a circular conversation where he brings it up again and again.

This is, according to Doug Edwards, the formula for handling a particular objection. I have practiced it and found that it works. If you have gained a level of sincerity with your customer and you put a problem area to bed, it never comes up to beat you over the head again.

I will number these specific objections for easy reference:

1. The Money Objection

Let's deal with more specific objections. Your first specific objection will normally be the money objection. The money objection usually presents itself in words such as, "Your product costs too much. I can't afford it. Somebody else will sell it to me cheaper." If you have never heard any of these money objections, then you certainly do not need to read this book.

In addressing the money objection, you will find that there are two basic ways to handle it. Let's see how they work. For example, say that you are selling an automobile, and your prospect says it costs too much. Your response is, "Of course it does, sir." What happens when you respond in this manner? It tends to confuse him. It throws him a little off base. You are not going to fight him.

Your next line is a question: "Tell me, sir, how much is too much?" And let's say he says $2,000. Your response is, "Great, sir. Let me ask you this question: How long do you anticipate that you would own this automobile?" Today in the automobile business financing goes up to seventy-two months, but let's say that he says five years. You say, "Great! Now how much would that be a year, sir? About $400 a year? That would be $33 a month, sir, or about $7.50 a week. And how much would that be a day, sir? About a dollar a day? And how many hours a day would you say that you would drive that car, sir?" Let's say his answer is two hours a day. "Now how much would that be an hour, sir? About 50 cents an hour – less than one penny a minute?"

You see what is happening here, don't you? When you reduce it to 50 cents an hour or one penny a minute that really is all you are talking about right now. And you say to your prospect, "The truth of the matter is that if you drive that car two hours a day—or maybe more because I know many people whose car is their office—you will be driving the car you want and the car that you and your family will be more comfortable in. You will actually take a sense of pride in owning it instead of the car that you are *forced* to settle for. Do you follow what I'm saying? This is what we are really talking about, sir, your true desire. Is that worth a penny a minute, sir? Is your personal comfort and pride worth one penny a minute? Here you pay less than a penny a minute for the car that you and *your family* will really enjoy and take pride in owning? Doesn't that make real economic sense to you, sir? Does that remove your concern?"

Edward Harding

What have you done? You have reduced it to the ridiculous! Now you *shut up* and allow him to make an ego conclusion in front of his wife and children. What you accomplished is to put *your* ego in your pocket and let him make a decision based on *his* ego. Is his ego and the car that his family really wants and will be proud of worth one penny per minute—or less than the price of a package of gum? Here I was redundant in order to emphasize the process of reducing his objection to a penny a minute.

> **Reduce it to the ridiculous!**

Now in this example I used bad words on purpose because I do not want to talk about investing 50 cents an hour or one penny per minute. What we did here was to *reduce it to the lowest common denominator*, in this case one penny per minute, and let him make an ego conclusion. Had he said that he would drive that car five hours a day, he would really be down to fractions of pennies. It would be, "Now, sir, is your own personal pride worth a quarter of a penny an hour?" Let him make an ego conclusion.

Can you use this on your product? When it comes to insurance, you can also reduce the cost to fractions of pennies. This also works really well for the real estate salesman whose prospect will be living in his house twenty-four hours a day, seven days a week for a possible 5-10 years. In fact, it works well on almost every product I have ever seen.

Here is another way to handle a money objection when your prospect again says that it costs too much. You say, "Absolutely, sir," and again you question, "How much too much?" Let's say it is a surround sound system and you are comparing a Bose with a lesser brand; you let him name it, and he says, "Five hundred too much!"

Again, take your ego, put it squarely in your back pocket, and say, "Sir, can I ask you this question? Isn't it true that every manufacturer has a choice to make? They may produce a product of superior quality and superior performance, or they may produce a product to do as little as it possibly can while having a decent name, sell it to the public as being just like a Bose. Now, I happen to know people who have spent $200,000 for the audio system in their home, but in the real world that you and I live in, we know that Bose makes the best product available for a reasonable cost. Now, why would the competition create a product that would do less than a Bose? Because it's cheaper. My family, just the same as yours, wants the product that does as much as possible instead of the one that does as little as it can get by with. Isn't that the way you feel, sir?"

While you have not fought him, you have demonstrated that he recognizes the superior product and can envision his family's enjoyment of it over the years—maybe $500 more doesn't mean so much over ten years. Do you see what I mean? Do you get the point? Do you follow me?

2. *The Competition Objection*

Competition is another area of objection to explore. The competition objection generally comes up in one of two ways. First, he's been buying it from his friend Ralph for ten years; why should he change now? Or another variable of the competition objection is that brand B is better. It is true many consumers have become loyal to brand names, product lines, people or companies, So let's attack both of these two monsters, one at a time.

> **Put *your* ego in your pocket and let him make a decision based on *his* ego.**

Knowing that loyalty is a tough nut to crack, we do not want to fight him here—or anywhere—so we have to provide some really solid answers. Let's say that you are a framing contractor approaching a general contractor who is building a spec house in a country club (this is going on because we know that a recession does not seem to affect the super wealthy people; they can still afford a second home on a golf course that might cost a couple of million dollars, and they are still spending money and because of the recession, they figure they can get a better price).

The general contractor says, "I've had Ralph as my framing contractor for ten years. He's done a great job for me so you might as well not waste your breath because I have no reason to change." Your response is, "Well, of course you're happy with Ralph, sir. I understand that completely, and I can respect your loyalty. May I ask you a question? How long have you been a general contractor building high-end homes?"

Let's say he says twenty years. "Then let me ask you another question, sir. When you made the change and hired Ralph, how many other framing contractors did you look at—at least three to five, right? What were the factors that made you choose Ralph over everyone else? Was there any benefit to you from the change you made when you chose Ralph? Why did you choose him at that particular time?"

What do you think he might say? Good attitude, worked harder, did a good job, superior quality work? What are we doing here? We are putting him in the position that he was in ten years ago when he hired Ralph. You must offer him superior advantages to what he is getting from Ralph. You must then point out to him both the situation and opportunity that existed then compared to the advantages he can gain by making a change today. We really could not *tell* him; we had to *ask* him. And we had to have him commit in his own words the advantages that he was looking for then and show him that we are willing to give him substantially more advantages today. Then we ask him if he can really afford to deny his company our benefits. In other words, maybe he would be wise to review his current options. "If our company will give you more benefits, including price, can we earn your business today?" Where can he go from here? You may have to close repeating your benefits ten or fifteen times in order to get him to take advantage of the benefits, including money.

Next let's talk about the second part of the competition objection: Brand B is better. You respond, "Of course I can understand why you feel that way about it, sir. You became acquainted with Brand B how long ago—two years ago? And you have found it very satisfactory, haven't you? Have there been any changes in Brand B in the last few years?"

What do you think he will say? "All products change." You answer, "That's true, and at the time you took on Brand B, you chose Brand B because in your good judgment, Brand B had made the largest number of changes that were in your interest, isn't that right? In other words, sir, what you wanted was not specifically Brand B; you wanted the greatest number of changes that were in your interest, isn't that right, sir? Are you still interested in the greatest number of changes in your interest?" Now you strongly recap and bullet-point the greatest number of changes that serve his interest!

> **Asking questions gives you information, and information is power.**

Where does he go? You didn't say Brand B was lousy. You brought him around to the greatest number of changes in his interest without fighting him. "Now, I'm sure that clarifies any competition from Brand B, doesn't it?"

There is a factor that I want to bring up here. I have not mentioned it before. I do not want to call it *question closing*, but I want to emphasize the importance of asking questions. When I was a little kid my grandmother was the real estate agent to all the movie stars. This is way back in the 1950's before Mike Silverman, before Coldwell Banker, before any large real estate firms had appeared in Los Angeles. In fact, my grandfather was president of the Beverly Hills Real Estate Board for three consecutive years—the only person to be president for three consecutive years!

Back to my grandmother… She used to take me with her, and I got to meet all the fabulous movie stars like Jane Mansfield, Marilyn Monroe, Bobbie Darin, and Sandra Dee. I was excited! It was great, but more importantly, I was watching the greatest *question closer* of all time. (Again, I hesitate to say *question close* because closing is the chapter we are going to get into next, but asking questions can be the secret and the key to your success.)

From the moment that my grandmother introduced herself, she was constantly asking questions and listening. Within twenty minutes she would know their whole life story, from their humble beginnings to their world famous status. By the end of the story, she would know exactly what they wanted. I cannot emphasize too strongly the power of asking questions. Asking questions gives you information, and information is power. My grandmother sold and rented more homes than any agent in Beverly Hills simply because of her down-home ability to be truly interested in people. She loved to work, and she sold her last house to Frank Sinatra's attorney at ninety years old.

> The basic method of handling the "location" objection is to change his base of thinking.

3. *The Location Objection*

Suppose your prospect inquires about the location of your factory from which he would order parts; he feels that it is too far away. Or the location where he has to make his investments is so far away that he is afraid that, because of the mail, his investment will be late or the home office or customer support location is too far. Did you ever hear any of these? I am sure that you have heard all of these objections, and the basic method of handling the "location" objection is to *change his base of thinking.*

Let's say your home office is in New York and you are talking to a prospect in Los Angeles. How would you *change his base of thinking*? First and foremost, bypass the objection, and if he brings it up again, simply ask this question, "Sir, isn't it true that today we live by time, not miles? Isn't that correct, sir? If you were to go from Los Angeles to New York, how far would it be approximately in miles—about three-thousand miles? How long would that take?" The answers to both of these questions are different, and they create a difference of opinion. One answer can be seven hours by plane, and the other answer can be five minutes by telephone, or, in the case of a more complicated negotiation, we now have video-conferencing.

The question is how do we measure distance today? We measure distance by *time*, not miles. For example, with video-conferencing, you can set up a video conference in five minutes. With Federal Express, you can have a part by 10:30 the next morning. "You see, sir, because of technology and the various one-day delivery services, distance is the least factor in business today. In fact, for the first time in history, we can setup a video conference any place in the world within minutes. Isn't that true, sir?"

Again, you must get him to say it, not just agree with it. If he has not said it and understood it, it just went in one ear and out the other. You have not overcome the objection. Suppose, depending on your product, you pose this question correctly and he understands that distance is nothing but a question of time. Then you confirm the answer to your objection. Be mindful that you must confirm the answer to the objection so that it is resolved in his mind and will not come up to beat you over the head again. Then ask for the order!

4. The Reputation And Past Experience Objections

Let us say that your prospect gives you an objection about your company. "I have done business with you before and my experience was not only unsatisfactory, it was down-right unpleasant." Or he says, "The representative you sent here last time was a bum and he offended me." How do you handle this?

Again, you do not fight him. I repeat, you do not fight him. You simply say, "I can understand how you would feel that way." You do not fight him. You simply say, "Let me ask you this question, sir? Did you ever have one of your clients come to you and point out a basic flaw in your product line? Or did you ever have one of your clients come to you and say an employee of yours is incompetent? In your entire history as a businessman, has this ever happened to you?"

What do you think he's going to say? These kinds of problems exist in every business, and it is your job to simply put the shoe on the other foot. When he says that he has experienced these problems in the past, you simply ask him, "What did you do about it, sir?" It does not make any difference what he says. Hear him out, and when he is finished you say, "That's what we did!" Where can he go from here? This will work, and it will work well because all companies have had certain problems, including this one. Your job is to psychologically put the shoe on the other foot.

This is especially true when he gives you the objection that the last representative you sent out was a bum. Make sure you ask him what he did with his employee in the same situation, and again you say, "That's what we did!" He has no place to go.

Repetition is the key in sales, so I will say again: simply ask him what he would do about the problem and enthusiastically say, "Well, that's what we did!" You have psychologically put the shoe on his foot. He will remember a situation and think of how he would have liked his prospect to respond to him. Nine times out of ten, he will respond to you the way he would like to have been treated. This objection is gone because he has no further point of argument.

5. *The Size Or Minor Objection*

Now we will address the *size* or *minor* objection. Your prospect says that it is too small, or it is too large, or is does not fit in a certain space. In the *minor* objection, you might hear, "If I could only get it with a longer warranty…" These objections are standard objections, and I am sure that everyone has been hit in the face with them. What do we do?

Again, sales creativity is critical because the creative salesperson is going to instantly know how to handle this objection, and again, we will rely on the response to the "location" objection. We simply *change his base of thinking* from *size to performance*. After demonstrating the superior performance of your product, no matter what the *size or minor objection*, if you have done a good job, you will bring him to the point where he is willing to make changes in his operation in order to gain superior performance, save time, and create a better product, and therefore, make more money. Isn't that what it's all about? We work for money in every business.

6. *The Third-Party Expert Stall*

You have just given a great presentation and answered all of your prospect's questions. You have buried all of his objections. But all of a sudden he says to you, "Well, it looks great to me, but before I make any decisions, I have to take it up with my attorney." Or if you are selling in heavy industry, he may say, "I have to take it up with my chief of operations or my head engineer." This objection can become difficult because it does not leave you much to get your teeth into.

Assuming you have given that great presentation and your prospect is really sincere and sold on your product, you simply say, "Now, sir, I want to ask you sincerely, have I satisfied you in every area?" If he says "yes," then you ask him about his attorney: "By the way, what's his telephone number?"

Why would you do this? Because you tell him that since you are driving in that direction now, perhaps he could call and let that person know that you're coming. But you have not yet nailed down this objection. Here is the key question: "Sir, am I right in assuming that the only reason I'm seeing this person is for is his authorization and agreement and that I have satisfied you completely; all you want is to have this person give me his formal recommendation and authorization, is that right?"

What do you think happens here? If he says *yes*, you've got the order. If he says no, you are going to ask why. When you are referred to someone else, you always put this third party into a position where he is merely an authorizing agent. To quote Doug Edwards here: "It's kill or cure, but it works." And never forget, you have a perfect right to fight for your order. Remember, the bottom line when you get to the real nitty-gritty is to "get them or forget them."

Edward Harding

In recapping, as you handle some of these minor detail objections such as location, past experience with products or representatives, or the day he might send in his monthly investment, how do you handle these things? You *change their base of thinking* from whatever the minor detail is to your greatest selling point, which eliminates the minor objection.

7. I'll Think It Over

If you have not heard "I'll think it over," then you have never really been in the sales business. This is probably the last objection that you are going to get because what he is really saying here is, "I've got nothing left to fight you with." This means that you have convinced him of the superiority of your product, you have answered all of his questions, and, basically, he has made his decision. But this last stall comes up, and it is a nasty one. The problem here, again, is that you have absolutely nothing to get your teeth into. What are you going to tell him? Are you going to tell him that he cannot take time to think it over? If you do, you are going to appear pushy and rude and make him angry. So here is what you do. You take "I want to think it over" and turn it into a closing opportunity which I will be covering in the next chapter on closes. Oh, don't you *hate* cliffhangers like this? But believe me, the wait is worth it.

> **Never forget, you have a perfect right to fight for your order.**

8. A Major Built-In Objection

The best method of handling a major objection that you know is built into your product is to **not** wait for him to bring it up; you *brag* about it first. Let's face it, every product has a built-in major objection, right? I do not care what product you are representing. You know that you have this one major built-in objection just waiting to come out and beat you over the head; and it is always there in the back of your mind. As a salesman, I know what you are going through. You are fortifying yourself to get hit with this objection, and you are seldom disappointed. How do you handle this? The secret and the key is to *brag about it*.

Find the positive aspect of this feature…and brag about it. You see, when you bring it up first and brag about it, nine times out of ten, he will never have the guts to object to it. Can you find a feature that outweighs this objection and brag about it first? Of course you can! When you do this first, I guarantee that you will knock out 60% of your problems in handling major built-in objections. You can do it; it just takes guts. Take this major objection, turn it into a feature, and brag about it.

Let's take an example. How about the new smart car? This car is so tiny and so flimsy that you know if you ever got into a major collision you would be seriously injured or dead. What has smart done? Marketing has taken this size objection and turned it into a "green," gas-saving, non-polluting feature, and they will tell you that they are the only manufacturers that understand the principle of the "green economy." We know that most Americans today love and want to hang on to their muscle car or SUV, but in this economy with gasoline prices climbing, getting eight miles to the gallon gives the smart car the ability to more than pay for itself in fuel consumption alone. Furthermore, they say it is a "green" product and kind to the environment. In many cases, the government will even give you a rebate for buying one.

Another example I have seen recently is an all battery-operated car which I shall refrain from naming. Not only does this automobile completely run on batteries, but it will do zero to sixty in 3.7 seconds! In other words, it will blow the doors off of a Mercedes 600SL and still give you the creature comforts you desire in a comfortable car such as power windows and air conditioning. It will go 240 miles on a single charge. Think about it. You pull your car into the garage and plug it into an electrical outlet they install. In a few hours it is completely charged and ready to go again, all on about the cost of four dollars of electricity. Imagine getting 240 miles per gallon with that kind of performance!

Edward Harding

There is one major objection. Because this is brand new technology, like any other new technology, it has a premium price of about $125,000. When I stopped to look at one, I found the sales force was very laid back and politically correct. They thought that just showing you the car would make it sell itself. Well, let me tell you, despite what you may have heard, *nothing sells itself.*

> **The best method of handling a major objection that you know is built into your product is to not wait for him to bring it up; you brag about it first.**

Again, as in any presentation, the salesperson must give a masterful "show" to the prospect. In the case of the automobile business, the first hurdle to jump is getting your prospect to test drive it. Once they see the way it handles and how it accelerates, you must overcome the "size" objection. For example, if Bob was driving this car to and from work every day, and let's say it takes two hours a day for an eighty to ninety mile round trip, the gas savings alone would almost pay for the car. And at the end of this rainbow you have a car that can go 240 miles for $4.00.

Another built-in objection might be that you cannot fill up at a local gas station, but the easy brag is that you can recharge the car in your own garage. I wonder why I have not seen any on the road yet. Could it be that the salesmen are not trained to really move cars?

Will this work in real estate? Of course it will! When you sell a home, you may notice a feature that may be less than popular. You must find a way to brag about this feature. Maybe it adds character to the house so that it doesn't have the ordinary tract home appearance. This could be effective when showing an older home such as the California Craftsman style home.

Today we know that many people have gone from single family residences to smaller homes such as condominiums or even mobile homes. Years ago nobody would have wanted these smaller dwellings. But smart real estate people have bragged about the modern American woman understanding the advantages of compact living. And, after all, don't all women want to be the modern American woman? And if you purchase a mobile home, the term itself suggests that you can move your home to a mobile home park wherever you choose to live.

Everyone knows that when you sell a house, the woman is the more influential decision maker. Believe me, she wears the pants in this area of major investments. Therefore, you must learn to brag about your built-in objection in a way that impresses "mom." As baby boomers get older, mom wants a home that doesn't require a ton of housekeeping. So when your property is smaller, you brag about less housework. Choose the feature that is least desirable and find a way to make it a positive feature…and then brag about it!

> **Despite what you have heard, nothing sells itself.**

Get The Tough Ones First! Terminate Objections!

We have now covered the process of handling objections. Again, I will reaffirm the basic theory: do not fight it; do not get involved in that process of the circular argument. Once you have buried an objection, make sure it never comes up again.

When I was a sales manager, I used to go out in the field with a trainee riding along with me so that he could learn to do what I did. I made it look easy—similar to watching a tennis pro hit the backhand with the right amount of spin on it to land it just over the net and then bounce sideways, automatically gaining him the point. He makes that look easy, but believe me, incredible backhands and amazing presentations take the repeated action of relentless practice until you can make it look easy.

When in the field with a trainee, I would give such great presentations that I would write orders and make it look so easy that it would seem like what we call a roll-over in the industry. When I'd walk out with the order in my pocket, my trainee would say, "I can't believe it! It was like watching a miracle. You just sold that expensive product without getting an objection."

Well, it was not a miracle. It was the result of practicing and fine tuning the methods I have given you here so that I eliminated objections…before they even came up. In handling objections, do not get lost in the process of fighting or arguing. Just answer the objections and confirm the answers. Eventually you will get to the point where you can eliminate objections in many of your presentations.

When I was new in the sales business, my grandmother told me that my grandfather had become the state agent for Penn Mutual Life Insurance Company, which meant that he got paid on every life insurance policy that was written in that state. I wanted to know how he had climbed to the top of the heap. She told me that he would wait until every salesman had gone out and talked to that tough old farmer (who lived in the boonies) and failed. Then he would go out…and write the order.

This made me think that if you learn to get the tough ones, the easier ones will fall into place automatically.

So I went in and asked my boss to give me all the orders that had cancelled on delivery. I would go out to the person's home unannounced and knock on the door and say, "Hi, I'm Ed Harding, and I'm here to deliver your product." The guy would look at me with tremendous irritation and say, "We cancelled that last night."

I'd immediately have a tantrum on his doorstep about the incompetence of the people that worked at our company, saying that if it was up to me I would fire them all. "And, by the way, would you mind if I used your phone so that I could give them a piece of my mind?" I knew that it would be amusing to him to watch me call the office and tell somebody off. While I was dialing the number or on hold for the person (who would never come to the phone), I'd turn to him and with all humility say, "By the way, what was the problem? Why did you cancel your order? Because basically I know we have a good product."

And he would tell me...boy, would he tell me. He would go through the list of objections I have reviewed in this chapter—and then some. Many times the customer would even say that he changed his mind or got buyer's remorse because he just didn't like the salesperson who was here before. Boy, was I happy to hear that because I knew I had the ability to make him like me! And I would simply turn around and say, "Oh my gosh, didn't he cover that?" I was right back in there selling. I learned to convert about 50% of all the cancellations.

> Amazing presentations take the repeated action of relentless practice.

So, remember, as you train yourself, if you can succeed with the hardest orders, the easy ones will fall into place without any objections. You will become number one in your crew and eventually number one in your whole company.

Earlier I told you that I did not want to get too deeply into closing techniques because I had dedicated a whole chapter to them. While you cannot lean on a single strong close and you must start closing *from the very beginning*, using many various closes masterfully can be the strongest technique you can use to increase your sales. Want to learn something that cost me hard work along with practice, practice, practice using J. Douglas Edwards' methods with perfection? Then keep reading, because I am about to instruct you on the art and power of the close.

Chapter 7

Closing the Sale

Before I begin this chapter, I would like to take a moment to acknowledge J. Douglas Edwards. Doug Edwards has been called the "Father of American Selling." Believe me, had I not studied his methods, I would have wasted years in achieving excellence and mastering the profession of selling.

We will be covering all the bases using his methods, along with my own observations, experiences, and examples—and we will do so without costing you thousands of dollars to get the information, which is really hard to find in one volume. Unfortunately, there is not even a biography of Doug Edwards on the Internet, which I think is a shame. I deeply respect Edwards and loved listening to his recordings when they were available, and one of the chief reasons is that he is very effective and his methods make sense—good common sense. They are so simple that you can adapt them to fit any presentation.

> **If you are not selling on commission, your income is not going to reach significant levels.**

Earl Nightingale's *The Strangest Secret*, made in 1956—another amazing instructional tool that I have listened to over and over and over, thousands of times—is still available through Nightingale-Conant, but Doug Edwards' CDs in his own voice are nowhere to be found. When they were, I listened to them so often and so many times that when I heard his voice, I felt like I knew him, that he was a friend.

To me, Edwards' strongest contribution to my sales technique was the close. Edwards once said, "*There is no subject on this earth that I am more happy to talk about than the subject called closing.*" Closing is where the art of selling becomes your masterpiece.

> **These closes are timeless classics, and they will fit into any presentation.**

I'm going to go ahead and make a bold statement: If you learn all of the closes contained in this book that worked for Edwards and me and practice them, even though they may seem old, you *will dramatically increase your sales*. These closes are timeless classics, and they will fit into any presentation. In some closes, the exact words are critical, so you must dedicate yourself to learning them. You must learn them inside and out until they become second nature.

Yet simply memorizing them is not enough; once you have committed them to memory, you must *put them into action*. You will only truly master the closes by taking action and using them. *Action* is the magic word! It will require action and practice to make these closing strategies truly conversational. Then you will experience the magic of the sales profession firsthand. If you become a master, you will teach many others to believe the way you and I have come to believe.

The Closing Instinct

First question: How many times do you take "no" for an answer before you give up? Be honest. Do you give up on the first "no," or the second "no"?

The truth is, when you look at a sales professional who earns a high six-figure income every year, you will find that you can use these great big-time pros' closing techniques, when practiced to perfection, in a completely conversational manner. This sets up the prospect so that he *does not even know he is being closed.* Those who master techniques to this level are the people who have transformed themselves from professionals into masters.

I have found that in closing the toughest sales I might have to close *ten to fifteen times*. When you realize there are so many salespeople who give up on the first or second "no," it is easy to see why so many people are afraid of selling on commission…and why many who are on commission are not making the money they could be. Believe me, if you are not selling on commission, your income is not going to reach a significant level.

> **The best way to learn how to close is by starting to close the minute you open your mouth.**

When I talk to people about closing, much like Doug Edwards, I find that salespeople ask me one question more than any other: "Ed, when do you close, and how did you learn how to close?" I have trained thousands and thousands of salesmen from New York to Hawaii, and I can tell you that the best way to learn how to close is by starting to close the minute you open your mouth. You may close too soon and too often, you may offend some prospects, or they may feel that you are pressuring them, but remember, you have nothing to be ashamed of. If you have a product you really believe in, you have a right to close that sale, go for the "tie-down" questions that are mini closes, and create strong commitments.

All the great salesmen I have met possess what is called a *closing instinct*. You do not have to tell them when to close. They know when to close, and they have learned to master their art *by closing* from the minute they open their mouths. By doing this, they *develop* the closing instinct.

Edward Harding

It really takes guts to close because this is where you run into one of the most fearsome of all emotions: rejection. Your prospect may very well turn you down, over and over. If you give a great presentation built on good, solid commitments, you have every right to ask your prospect to okay your agreement or authorize your purchase order because he has told you over and over again when you were getting those commitments how much he would use the product. In closing, you will go back to those major commitments many times.

When you start to close from the beginning, your prospect has already agreed many times how beneficial it would be to his business. He might reflexively say "no," but if you have closed from the start, you know he really wants or needs what you are presenting. Closing under the pressure of rejection is what it takes to become a master.

So let us examine the basic close by breaking it down one piece at a time so you, too, can learn to have a closing instinct. In fact, I have numbered the closes 1-13 for easy reference.

1. Order Blank Close

The *order blank close* is always the number one close. Every sales person who has mastered the art of selling and who is creating those money-earning masterpieces is using the *order blank close*. This close is a basic element. You cannot succeed without it. When you use the *order blank close*, you can flow right into it. Much of the information you may already have, but you must get your prospect to start answering the questions. All you have to do is ask your prospect questions; it is really quite simple.

You fill out the answers on your order blank, purchase order, agreement, credit application, or whatever your closing form is. Never ask, "Can we go ahead?" Just start asking questions and putting the responses on your order blank.

What kind of questions do you ask? Obviously, you must start with your prospect's correct full name and address. Keep going through the form, asking one question after another, realizing that as long as he does not stop you, *he has bought*. This is also *assumptive closing*.

This is the secret—you assume that he has bought; you are just filling out the form. When you get the whole form completed, simply swing it around and ask him to *"okay"* it or authorize it. Remember what we discussed about language—never ask him to sign it. We have gone over this before because all our lives we have been told not to "sign" anything—we are taught to read it, be careful, and beware. He, too, has been told not to sign anything. So, once again, he will not "sign" it, but he will "okay" it, or "authorize" it or "autograph" it.

Many times I put my pen on top of the order blank, and as I handed it to him, the pen fell right into his lap or on to his desk. He picked it up, and there he was, pen in hand ready to okay my agreement. He had already bought.

Learn When To Shut Up

The next instruction I am going to give you is the most critical instruction you will ever hear in the art of closing. If you want to be a big-time closer, you must remember certain fundamentals.

Do you understand what a closing question really is? A closing question is any question the answer to which confirms the fact that your prospect has bought. Again, go back to your order blank: His correct full name, mailing address, and anything else on there are all closing questions.

So are you ready for the critical instruction? If you listen to me, you can make incredible wealth, but if you choose not to follow this direction, you will always remain a clerk. Whenever you ask a closing question—and I repeat, *whenever you ask a closing question...*

Shut Up! Shut Up! Shut Up!

Edward Harding

Remember this: The first person who talks loses; and this is universally true. After you have asked the closing question, *shut up*.

I remember Doug Edwards told a story about conducting a training session for a big New York corporation. The president of the company walked in just as he was screaming at the top of his lungs, "Shut up!" Edwards said that the president of the company jumped about a foot in the air, turned around, and walked out of the room. Doug said that every time his telephone rang he felt nervous because he thought that by telling salesmen to shut up, he might get fired. But as he continued to tell the story, the following week while he was conducting the same seminar to the same corporation, the boss walked in at exactly the same moment—this time not budging—and asked Doug if he would mind if he interjected a little story.

> **The first person who talks loses.**

Who was he to say "no" to this man? So the president of this big corporation began speaking, stating that he had heard what Doug said last week. The president said that it amused him, so he thought he would try it. He said he just had a salesman in his office trying to lease him a product that was going to cost a million dollars a year—and this is back in the 1950's.

He said this salesman must have been well-trained because when he asked the closing question, he shut up, "And, Douglas, so did I," the president said. "We sat there for twenty minutes in dead silence. You know what happened? I laughed, and I bought." Doug Edwards tells this story to illustrate that here was a young man in the 1950's—when a million dollars was *really* a million dollars—and his million dollar sale hung on a silent close. He had already sold the president; he just had to shut up and get the sale.

The first person who talks is the one who loses. Edwards illustrates the wisdom of shutting up after asking a closing question in reverse by showing how the prospect actually shut up and still bought because he was the first one to laugh. Try it out. Ask anybody anything…and shut up. You will find that people cannot stand ten seconds of silence without opening their mouths. Talk about pressure! There is no greater pressure you will ever exert or experience than the *pressure of silence.*

It is important to recap the tremendous pressure you can exert by asking a closing question and shutting up. You can also call this a *silent close.* Using the silent close takes guts! Imagine, you ask a closing question…and shut up. I don't care how long it takes.

> **There is no greater pressure you will ever exert or experience than the pressure of silence.**

Doug Edwards cites an example of a salesman who got a million dollar a year order by shutting up for twenty minutes! Those twenty minutes must have seemed like an *eternity*! I challenge you to try the silent close. Ask your closing question and *shut up*. What could possibly happen? Your prospect will either go along with you, ask you a question, or give you an objection. Whatever happens, you are trained to handle it, aren't you?

The other day I was recruiting a young couple who had the highest integrity, honor, and desire to do the right thing. When I asked them if they would consider being high-pressure salespeople—a goal that would result in making them rich—they immediately responded, "No." The high pressure, suede shoe, slick con-artist type was not what they wanted to be.

I replied, "Well, let's take this pressure thing and look at it from a more pragmatic viewpoint. In today's world, your prospect is not going to be convinced by using high-pressure tactics." I told them that they needed to stop and think about it for a minute. We all agree that when we take many of the basic direct selling methods of the past and re-design them to fit into today's world, we cannot make money, be successful, and do all the good things we have in our hearts unless we get the order *now*.

Edward Harding

As I said earlier, if you do not acquire that prospect as a customer, you will never see him again. He will not come back to you with repeat business because you did not persuade him or create the relationship in the first place. Would you say that this is true or false? They agreed that it was true because they understood that you must close the sale in order to create the relationship.

> **Professional closing methods and techniques transcend generations.**

I told them that the greatest form of pressure that they could ever exert on their prospect was *shutting up after asking the closing question*. In that period of silence, the pressure builds up. It is the greatest pressure a salesperson can use to his advantage in a closing situation. I asked them if they would have an ethical problem asking the closing question and then *shutting up*, hence creating the highest form of pressure, silence. "Would you consider that a violation of your moral code?" I asked.

These folks said, "No." They agreed that using the pressure of silence after asking the closing question was moral and honorable and would not violate their personal integrity. I immediately stated, "You see, you just became high-pressure salespeople!" A big smile broke out on both of their faces as they instantly "saw the light" and understood that their use of silence not only raised them to a higher level of professionalism but was also in line with their ethical code. When recruiting young people into the profession of selling, the desired result is that they have an epiphany that raises their consciousness from the old ideas of the "high-pressure" selling into 21st century methods of closing the sale. The basic closing methods transcend generations and even centuries. Remember, there is no pressure you will ever exert as powerful as silence.

2. *The Alternate of Choice Close*

There are all kinds of alternates of choice: Are you going to buy this way, or are you going to buy that way? The only word I object to is the word *buy*. Naturally, you would start the *alternate of choice* close by asking a question. This question must be prefaced by, "Which would you prefer?" Then you give him a choice. For example, "Would you prefer to use your pen or mine?"

What are some other *alternates of choice* you can give your prospect?

    A. "Which do you prefer, the three- or the four-year plan?"

    B. "Which do you prefer, cash or credit card?"

    C. "Do you prefer the premium feature upgrade or the standard features?"

    D. "Do you want your premiums monthly or annually?"

    E. "Which color do you prefer—black or white?"

    F. "Would you prefer the extended warranty or the factory warranty?"

    G. "Which would you prefer, the classic look or the newest style?"

I have just given you seven examples that are somewhat generic. How many *alternates of choice* can you think of that apply specifically to your product?

You better think of as many as you can. The reason is that the *alternate of choice* is the premier assumptive close. Here you don't ask if he is *going* to buy; you *assume* it. Do you realize that the minute he makes a choice, he has bought? You don't ask for his decision to buy—you assume that it has been made. This close is so assumptive that it can create a miracle.

When I first used this close, I did not have much faith that it would get me orders. When I asked, "Which would you prefer, the three-year plan or the four-year plan?" the prospect would simply say, "The three-year plan." There were also instances where my prospect would say that he wanted the one-year plan or even planned on paying cash; this was great because the shorter the plan, the stronger the order.

In fact, for me this close was so powerful and so assumptive that when I asked, "Would you prefer to use your pen or mine?" the prospect would simply take the pen I held out to him and okay the agreement. Remember to preface this close with, "Which would you prefer?"

3. *The Negative Close or Takeaway*

This is an extremely powerful close, which I did not learn from Doug Edwards. As a matter of fact, I never really liked it because in the negative close, you take the product away from the prospect and tell him that he cannot have it unless he qualifies for it. In order to get the benefit of whatever extra bonus is tucked into your product, your prospect must demonstrate that he will use it. *Positive closing demands that you simply remind your prospect of his communication; ask if he was being sincere. When he says "Yes," you've got him*! Where can he go without admitting that he lied?

> **Even though I have said that sales is psychological, I do not think it is good psychology to evade the truth.**

I never much liked negative closing or the *takeaway close* because it always reminded me of the old "suede shoe" salesman of the 1950's and 1960's who would use the advertising close and tell you that you could have the product free if you would advertise for their company, recommending your friends by providing them with three qualified leads per month over a three year period. With a closing average of one out of three, these three qualified leads could get the company at least twelve new sales a year. The pitfall was that the prospect could never produce three qualified leads a month and would end up having to make the monthly payments.

These methods of closing were always offensive to me. I like a positive, straightforward, honest close…that goes right for the throat. Even though I have said that sales is psychological, I do not think it is good psychology to evade the truth. I find it offensive and dishonest. One of the reasons that some of these closes no longer exist is that they became so dishonest that the company would end up having complaints filed with the Attorney General. Consequently, you could find yourself sitting in front of Herschel Elkins, Senior Assistant Attorney General, explaining your dishonesty or misrepresentation.

> **If you do not ask for the order, you will never get it.**

Let me just add that this certainly does not mean that just because you have a few complaints and get investigated by the Attorney General that you work for a bad company. All companies have complaints. In fact, there is an old saying, "Anything that moves creates friction." And I will tell you that I have been to the Attorney General's office. Let's face it. When you are in charge of hundreds of salesmen, you cannot follow them around and make sure that they give a straight presentation. Any company getting between five to ten complaints will most likely end up with an attorney general investigation, depending on the merits of the complaint.

I do not believe that Herschel Elkins is still around in the Los Angeles office of the Attorney General of the State of California. In fact, I am sure he is not, but I can tell you that, even though you may look at him as a state bureaucrat, he put some big direct-marketing companies out of business because their tactics were dishonest (and truthfully) because salesmen can sometimes misrepresent an honest presentation. For example, whenever you see anything that boasts a lifetime guarantee, you should understand that there is a seven-year statute of limitations on any guarantee. It is illegal to tell anyone that he is getting something for free—unless it is *absolutely* free. The language you should be using is, "included *at no additional cost.*"

Edward Harding

The same message is being conveyed, but believe me, the Attorney General will view it very differently.

I remember the first time I sat in front of Herschel Elkins. My mentor and boss, Joe Martin, told me that he was going to show me how to handle this situation one time and that I should never put myself in a position where I was called before the Attorney General. When we went up to visit good old Herschel, Joe told me that the only power he had was given to him by the state. He said that was plenty, and he asked me if I was afraid. When I said no, he told me that I was a fool.

When we went to see the Attorney General, he gave Joe about a five-minute tongue-lashing. Then Joe diplomatically butted in and reminded him that he had been in business for over a decade and had never committed a violation. Mr. Elkins acknowledged that, and the meeting went on amicably with him merely reminding us of the rules of the road. Some time later I had to go before the Attorney General myself, and, fortunately, I had included in our paperwork a disclaimer authorized by every customer stating that our company complied with certain requirements that existed at that time. Because I had the foresight to make sure my bases were covered—and by the way, I had only three complaints for the hundreds of salesmen I had in California—Mr. Elkins actually *commended* me for the good job we were doing.

Like I said, there is no way any sales manager can know what every salesperson out in the field is saying to each customer. That is up to the individual salesperson. Throughout this book I have made a big point of telling you to put yourself in a position where you have a right to expect to get your order, or, at the very least, that you have earned the right to *ask* for your order. I must tell you that if you lie, cheat, misrepresent, or take short cuts to get an order, you will be in business a very short time. It does not make any difference how big your company is or what your product is. Many large companies find themselves out of business when they misrepresent themselves or conduct business in gray areas. To be a professional, you must decide for yourself how you are going to represent your company and your product. It is a good idea to always under promise and over deliver. If you conduct yourself with integrity and you follow the legitimate methods of influence in this book, *you will win.*

FEAR: *False Evidence Appearing Real*

The *fear of rejection* is a canard (a deliberately misleading fabrication) that keeps people who enter the profession of selling from making progress. This is a subject that I will probably touch on several times as we go through various closing techniques. One thought that always saved me as I evolved into a professional was remembering what my boss told me incessantly. I pass it on to you: *You cannot lose something you do not have.*

It reminded me of the lyrics from an old Bob Dylan song that said, "When you ain't got nothin', you got nothin' to lose." When you reach the point in your presentation where it is time to ask for the order, remember, go ahead and ask. You have earned the right to ask for that order by giving a great presentation. *If you do not ask for the order, you will never get it.* Take that negative ego that is so delicate that it cannot handle a little rejection and put it in your back pocket—for now. I promise you that if you just sit there and wait for your prospect to say, "Okay, we'll take it" without closing, you will *never* make the sale and you will remain a peon in the sales business. Always remember—in fact repeat it in your head as a mantra—"I can never lose what I haven't got, I can never lose what I haven't got…"

4. The "Puppy Dog" Close

This is one of the all time great closing devices. Do you know how you sell a puppy dog? Let the people take it home overnight. After it has been in their home and they have loved it and played with it and the neighbors have come in and seen it, they can *never* bring it back. This is so simple and probably the most frequently used close today.

When Doug Edwards talks about the *puppy dog close* he tells a story about a small mid-western appliance dealer who sold more color television sets in 1963 than anyone else in America. He did a lot of good advertising designed to bring people into his store. When they came in, they always looked at a color television set. Then he would walk up to them and say, "I imagine you're wondering if your family could live with one of those things, aren't you? You know there are a lot of families that just can't get along with color television sets. I'll tell you what I'll do. I wouldn't let you have one of these unless I knew that you and your family could live with it. I'm going to send one out. It's not going to cost you a dime. I'll send it out and you can take a look at it. What's your address?" He would then deliver the television set to them. This guy actually contradicted everything that Doug Edwards taught because *he never closed*. Three days after sending the set out, he would telephone them and ask, "Can I come out and readjust the set? Is it operating alright?" His prospect was expecting a close but did not get one. Then the salesman left them alone, but in less than two weeks the "prospect" would come into his store and ask, "How do I go about paying for that darned thing?"

Why did he do this? Why did he make the effort to come in and want to buy it? He told the salesman it was because all the kids in the neighborhood had been to his home to see that color television. All his friends did the same thing. Could they now say that they sent it back? This is puppy dog closing.

I do not know if I can even cover the many ways in which the *puppy dog close* is used in today's marketing. Ads on television claim a 30-day free home trial—if you don't like it, just send it back, and we'll give you a refund with no questions asked. You see, today's version of the *puppy dog close* puts the prospect in the position where he has nothing to lose. He can try it out, and if he likes it, he keeps it. If he doesn't like it, he just returns it and gets his money back. Returning it rarely happens. What could be simpler? Today we sell everything from record collections, cosmetics, health devices, and countless other products all the way up to *fifty million dollar gulf-stream jet planes* using the *puppy dog close*. Almost every product has some part of the *puppy dog close* incorporated within its closing methodology.

Years ago I was interviewing distributors for a direct marketing product. In came this fellow; he was past middle age and kind of paunchy, and to tell the truth, he really did not look like dealer material. As I looked at his resume, I saw that he had been the national sales manager for *Encyclopedia Britannica*. This meant that he was a heavyweight professional master of persuasion as well as a great leader who would have earned a seven-figure income. While I chatted with him, I asked what he was doing at that time. He stated that he was semi-retired and owned a farm in central California. He also indicated that he was doing some consulting for a firm called McDonnell-Douglas. Boeing bought out McDonnell-Douglas years ago, but in those days, Douglas Aircraft designed, manufactured, and sold everything from DC-10s to Air Force fighters and transport planes.

> **Most people just answer the question instead of using the question as an opportunity to confirm the sale.**

When I inquired as to what kind of consulting he did for McDonnell-Douglas, he told me that he ran weekly training seminars for their sales force. I was flabbergasted. Here I was, thirty-eight years old, thinking I was the best there was, and this old guy comes in and tells me that he is teaching salesmen to sell DC-10 commercial jets as well as aircraft to the defense department. These sales had to be anywhere from one hundred million to *several billion dollars*.

I asked him, "How could an old book salesman train people to sell something as sophisticated as the DC-10 or fighter planes?" I guess I was just an arrogant young punk because this old fellow reminded me that it does not make any difference whether the product is an encyclopedia or the most sophisticated aircraft the US defense department uses. He said that the methods and sales strategies were all the same. A truism you will find as we proceed, beginning with the order-blank close to some of the more sophisticated closes, is that you can adapt simple, basic, closing techniques like the puppy dog close to any product sold in America today. You will be able to tell your prospect that he has absolutely nothing to lose. You will then build a great relationship for repeat orders.

5. *The Sharp Angle Close*

This is an amazing yet simple close that anyone who works on commission selling shoes, real estate, insurance, or business services of any kind can use immediately. Consider the saleswoman who sells high-end designer products at Nordstrom's. A customer approaches and asks, "Does this dress come in red?" What should her answer be? When I ask most people this question they respond, "Yes, we have it in red." What a perfect example of why there are so many mediocre salespeople because they fail to demonstrate excellence in their techniques. The objective should be to tie down the sale by simply asking, "Did you want it in red?" Upon producing the dress in red you take it up to the counter and consider the sale completed. Of course you will want to suggest accessories to complement the outfit and "up sell" in any creative manner that fits the product.

This is an example of the *sharp angle close*. It also works in many other areas. When a customer asks, "Will it do this or that?" You "sharp-angle" him by asking, "Do you want it if it does?" This *sharp angle close* can be used whether you are selling a multi-level marketing cosmetics line or you are a real estate agent selling a new home. This close is so simple, yet it is so overlooked in today's market place. Most people just answer the question instead of using the question as an opportunity to confirm the sale. Confirming the sale is the *sharp angle close*.

6. *The Benjamin Franklin Balance Sheet Close*

I love this close! I found that when I mastered this close, it added hundreds of dollars a week to my income. When I first began to use the *Benjamin Franklin Balance Sheet Close*, I fumbled around because, while it is fairly simple, you must be a bit of an actor and have the sequence of words in an exact order. This is also somewhat of a "story" close to be used on that prospect who is just wishy-washy or indecisive. Use it when you cannot nail him down, and you cannot seem to figure out why. One thing is for certain. You will either get the order or you will not, and there is no question that you definitely *want* that order. And people love stories!

The words and their order in this close are critical. It is a "story" close and it goes like this: "I'm sure you folks know that in America we have long considered Benjamin Franklin to be one of our wisest founding fathers. He discovered electricity. He helped write the *Declaration of Independence* and the U.S. Constitution that created the Republic of the United States. A lesser known fact is that he was also one of America's first millionaires." (As an aside, you will see his face on my favorite bill, the hundred-dollar bill.)

"When Old Ben found himself in a situation similar to what you're in today, he felt pretty much the way you feel. If it was the right thing to do, he wanted to make sure and do it. If it was the wrong thing, he wanted to make sure and avoid it. *Isn't that exactly the way you feel right now?*" When the prospect says yes, proceed by saying, "Here's what Old Ben used to do." He would take a sheet of plain white paper and draw a line right down the middle." Now you take a sheet of plain white paper and draw a line right down the middle. "On one side he would write 'Yes,' and on the other side he would write 'No.'" As you point to the "Yes" side, say, "He would list all the reasons favoring his decision today." And then pointing to the "No" side, say, "Then he would write down all the reasons against it. When he was finished, he would simply compare the number in the 'Yes' column to the number in the 'No' column, and his decision was made for him. Why don't we try it and see what happens?"

Example	
Yes For	No Against
1.	1.

Edward Harding

2.	2.
3.	3.

Next you hand your prospect this sheet of paper and your pen and say, "Let's see how many reasons we can think of in favor of your decision today." This is where you give him all the help in the world. "How about this?" "How about that?" "How about this other thing?" You give him all the ideas he needs. You keep on going and if you are any kind of a salesperson, you can add at least twenty reasons to the "Yes" side.

When you get to the "No" side say, "Let's see how many reasons you can think of against your decision today." *And you shut up!* When you use this close effectively, your prospect will not be able to think of more than four or five reasons for the "No" side. Think about it. Have you ever had a prospect write down—in his own handwriting—why he should buy your product today? Has this ever happened to you? That is what happens here. He is doing the writing. Do you realize what is happening to his mind? You coach him on the "Yes" side, and he cannot switch fast enough to think up his own reasons for the "No" side. Next all you have to do is start counting, "One, two, three…twenty-four. Okay! We've got twenty-four on the 'Yes' side. Let's see how many we have on the 'No' side. One, two, three… Well, the answer is kind of obvious, don't you think?"

Keep it flowing and hand him a copy of your simple agreement. Ask him to okay it for you. This is a great close! It works! But you absolutely must include the reference to Benjamin Franklin. As an aside, you can find this information in *Poor Richard's Almanac*.

7. *The Summary Question Close*

This is what we call a "Negative-Yes" close because in this close, you allow your prospect to say "No." But every time he says "No," he really means "Yes." The objective of this close is to rapidly eliminate any objections to making the purchase today.

It usually starts out with the salesperson saying, "Just to clarify my thinking, sir, what is it that is not quite clear to you? Is it the integrity of (name your company)? Is it my personal integrity?"

He will say, "No." But remember, the "No" really means "Yes" to the sale, because each thing he agrees to is a reason for him to purchase. Keep going down the list of all the significant bullet points of your presentation one question at a time: "Is it this?" "Is it that?"

The last thing you get to is money, which, by the way, is all the way down the list. Remember, every time he said, "No" to you, he really meant "Yes." Didn't he?

By the time you get all the way to the bottom, if he says, "Yes" to money, you have a final objection, don't you? Assuming you know the answer to the objection, you question him: "Just to clarify my thinking, sir, you already stated that you were going to get the product and it certainly would be of use to you. So money is not really the issue, is it, sir, because you're going to invest in the product whether from me or from somebody else? Isn't that true, sir? I would certainly like to have the chance to earn your business." Now you swing the contract around again. Put the pen in his hand and ask him to authorize the purchase order or agreement.

8. *The Similar Situation Close*

This close is an old favorite of the insurance industry. Every big-time high-producing insurance sales pro uses it. This close can certainly be expanded beyond the insurance industry and applied to almost any product. The problem today is that in selling, or what the politically-correct call marketing, we have lost some of these old tried-and-true methods. When this close was primarily used in the insurance industry, it was labeled the "back-the-hearse-up-to-the-door-and-let-them-smell-the-roses close." It was also called the "make-them-cry-close," or described as the "make-them-wish-that…close."

The *similar situation close* can apply to any product. It does not have to have a negative connotation to make it work. Here I will show you how it was used in the insurance industry. And, once again, this is a reference taken directly from J. Douglas Edwards. You have probably had an insurance salesman use this close on you. Here is how it goes: "You know, Mr. and Mrs. Jones, just a couple of weeks ago I was sitting in a home just down the block here with a young couple. I was trying to make a presentation to them about how critical insurance was to their very lives. They had a little daughter, I'd say three or four years old. A little blonde kid. Real cute. The first thing she did was climb into her father's lap, but he shoved her off. Then she climbed into her mother's lap, but she shoved her off. The next thing I knew she was climbing up onto my lap, and here I was trying to give a presentation about insurance to her parents. I couldn't shove her off, but her mother finally came to my rescue. She picked up this little girl, spanked her little behind and said that she was going to get a time-out in her room. The little girl was crying all the way out of the room.

Well, I didn't sell insurance to those people that night. And you know just yesterday morning I picked up the newspaper and cried because that mother and father had just been killed in an automobile accident. I am haunted by this, not because of the mother and father, but all I can think of is that little girl who was so desperate for affection that she crawled into the lap of a stranger."

You can see that the salesperson was providing a similar situation to illustrate the significant effect of his failure to sell those people insurance that night which would have protected the little girl's welfare and education. When you use this close in a similar situation, it is very difficult for the prospect to refuse you without tacitly admitting that they do not love their child.

Just as effective is the similar situation in which you define a person's happiness because he did own your product. There is no reason in the world why any salesperson cannot tell a story about someone who decided to invest in the product and achieved a happy unexpected result.

Now I will tell you how I used this close to achieve many sales when I was selling cassette tapes. I recorded my grandmother's voice on a cassette tape. She had since passed away, and I carried this cassette tape with me in my sales kit. She described her 19th century lifestyle and all the wonderful changes that took place in the world. She brought to life the adventures she had experienced during her 96 years. I would play a portion of this tape for my prospects.

> **If the prospects have the need and desire, and if they don't buy, it is your fault, not theirs.**

I would then ask them, "If you had a copy of your grandmother's voice on tape just as I do and you could not replace it because she had passed on, would you sell me the tape for five thousand dollars?" Nine times out of ten the prospects would say, "No." I would say, "You see, I have just shown you how a $1.50 blank cassette tape can be worth five thousand dollars to you. I ask you, Mr. and Mrs. Jones, 'Can you afford not to invest in our program?'" Next I simply handed them the agreement and asked them to okay it.

What I have done here is use a similar situation to create nostalgia that was worth five thousand dollars. Believe me, this close increased my weekly income. In similar situation closing we relate stories about someone who made the right decision and was commended for making it. Therefore, the prospect thinks that if he, too, makes that same right decision, he will gain praise or gratitude for it.

Why should this close be limited to the insurance industry? It can be adapted to just about any product. I adapted it to the cassette tape business. There is no reason why a salesperson cannot tell a story about a *similar situation* and put the prospect in the shoes of that good decision-maker.

The similar situation close is a story close. *People love stories*! It is unfortunate that it seems we are losing our story-telling ability as part of the selling process because people really do love stories.

Edward Harding

9. *The Call Back Close*

It has been my experience that there is no such thing as a good *call back close*. The rule in sales is: *You either get them or forget them.* Your goal is to get the order from your prospect *today*. Nevertheless, I am going to guide you in the best way I know of to handle a *call back close* if you must. When your prospect says to you, "You'll have to come back tomorrow and meet with my partner," you have no choice but to acquiesce and make that appointment for tomorrow. When you arrive the next day for that call-back appointment, you start out by saying, "I'm very sorry, sir, but yesterday when I was here there was something I forgot to tell you. I think it's important." No matter what it is, just tell them something new ("It's going to get warmer in the desert." Say whatever, so long as it is something new.) This act enables you to regain control of the situation.

After you give him the new information, tell him you want to review all of the information you went over the day before. Now give him the whole presentation all over again! The whole presentation! The only difference today is that you pepper your presentation by occasionally saying, "As you remember...", "You will recall...", "We said that...", "You agreed that..." But you must give him the whole presentation and go into a normal closing sequence.

Many times a prospect will say, "I want to think it over." You come back the next day and, like a dummy, you say, "Well, did you think it over?" He replies, "Yes... No." This is the horrible consequence of the *call back close.* Never ask if he thought it over. *Telling him something new is the secret to the call back close.* Give the whole presentation again and close him and his partner at the same time. *But do not ever ask if he thought it over.* Later in the chapter we will go into more detail regarding the "I'll think it over" response. I will show you how to transform this objection into a powerful close.

10. *The Lost Sale Close*

This close is what it says it is. Use the *lost sale close* when you reach the point in the presentation where you have lost the sale. Either he is red in the face with his fists clenched or you ran out of energy and quit. This lost sales close is pretty basic and has been around for years.

Here's how it goes. Your prospect is angry and telling you to get out of his house or you have given up. You pack up and head for the door. Just as you get to the door you turn around and say, "Pardon me, sir. I wonder if you would help me for a moment? *Before I go, I would like to apologize to you for being so inept a salesperson.* You see, if I had been able to make you feel like I feel about (for example, this home) you would have owned it by now. Your children would be planning to play in the new backyard. You and your wife would be planning to swim in the pool and relax in the Jacuzzi. But now your children aren't going to have this yard to play in or this pool to swim in. You're not going to have this Jacuzzi to relax in. Your wife is going to have to keep cooking in that old kitchen and cleaning that old house. And I want you to know that it is completely my fault, and I'm truly sorry. As you may realize, this is how I make my living and support my family. I want to make sure that I don't make the same mistake again. Would you mind telling me what it is that I did wrong?"

> **Before I go, I would like to apologize for being such an inept salesperson.**

And believe me, he will gladly tell you what you did wrong! Then you reply, "Oh-h-h-h, didn't I cover that?" And now you are right back in there and on course to closing on the objections the prospect gave you. But a word of caution—you may have never before apologized to a prospect for being so inept a salesperson. You probably should have apologized because if there is a need or use for your product combined with the purchasing capacity, you should have made the sale. If he did not buy, it is your fault! Don't go around blaming stupid prospects. This is the fault of a stupid salesperson.

Edward Harding

If the prospects have the need and desire, if they qualify, and if they don't buy, it is your fault, not theirs. And you ought to apologize. By the way, this apology and asking them to tell you what you did wrong will lead you to a final objection or perhaps a couple of objections. This works, but let me tell you something—when you make this apology, you had better be *completely sincere* because they have to *believe* it. If you come across insincere or "cute," your prospect will know it and throw you out on your butt. On the other hand, if your apology is truly sincere you may find that this *lost sale close* technique actually gets you the sale!

11. The Secondary Question Close

In teaching you the *secondary question close*, I am going to quote J. Douglas Edwards word for word because, as I see it, this close is not outdated, and his analysis is the best way to explain it. "A good friend of mine who was a salesman of mine was selling an intangible business service—the toughest product in the world to sell, tougher than insurance, tougher than advertising. The toughest of all the intangibles is business services. He used to use this *secondary question* close, and he used to use it magnificently! He used to use it like this. At the point of sale, he would say to a man, 'As I see it, sir, the only decision you have to make today is do you want this for the two- or the three-year term? By the way, do you want to use your pen or mine?' "

Why is this a great close? This is as great a close as you will ever hear. What did he do? Read it again carefully. Sure, there was an alternate of choice there, but it was not a simple alternate of choice, was it? Here is what he did: He posed the major question, "Now as I see it, sir, the only decision you have to make today is do you want this for the two- or the three-year term?" But he did not give the man a chance to decide, did he? He immediately followed it with a minor decision, "By the way, do you want to use your pen or mine?" You realize that when your prospect makes the minor decision, the major decision is carried, isn't it? This is secondary question closing at its finest. You pose the major question, but before he has a chance to answer, you immediately follow with a minor alternative of choice. When he makes the minor alternate, the major alternate automatically carries. This may seem simplistic, but believe me, I have used this close and watched it work like a miracle. This is where you are doing brain surgery without a scalpel.

12. *Closing On A Final Objection*

We are now going to address the two most important closes you will probably ever use. *Closing on a final objection* and *"I'll think it over."* J. Douglas Edwards always called this his "$100,000 combination" because if you use them, your annual income will increase by at least $100,000 a year. Anyone who does not need an extra $100,000 a year might as well close this book and put it on the shelf.

> **Do not make the mistake that every salesman makes of hearing three words and assuming you know what the prospect is going to say.**

Let me set the stage for you. Normally when you ask your first closing question the prospect seldom says, "No." Normally the prospect gives you an objection. Isn't that right? What do you do? You answer the objection. Does this get you a close? All it does is create another objection. Now here you are in this death-mill of salesmen. Can the prospect think of more objections than you can answer, or can you answer more than he can think of? As fast as you neutralize each objection, up comes another. After you have answered objection after objection, the prospect will go back to the original objection. You get into a fruitless, endless, circular conversation because you did not button up the answer to each objection that arose earlier by saying, *"Now that covers that completely, doesn't it, sir?"*

Follow this formula to make that *first* objection the *last* one. I quote J. Douglas Edwards because his formula is basic and timeless.

Step 1: Hear them out.

Step 2: Sell them their objection.

Step 3: Confirm the objection.

Step 4: Question it.

Step 5: Answer it.

Step 6: Confirm the answer.

Step 7: Close it.

Let us now begin to get more detailed by adding my own four decades of experience.

Listen. Do not make the mistake that every salesman makes of hearing three words and assuming you know what the prospect is going to say. Do not jump in and answer what you think he is going to ask or say. Even if you guess right, he is going to be irritated. And the odds are that you will not guess right.

After you have listened to his objection, sell it to him. How do you sell it to him? You expand it and look defeated. It is important that you look licked. Again, you must be an actor.

Question it by saying, "As I understand it, sir, the price of this car is just more than you feel you can afford to invest in an automobile." You look defeated; you have already expanded it, and now you will confirm it. "Now, sir, this _is_ the only thing standing between us, isn't it? If this car that you want for yourself and your family cost a little bit less, you'd go along with me today, wouldn't you, sir?"

If you still look defeated, he will probably go along with you and may even jump right in and take the bait. He may tell you, "Sure, I like the car and my family would love the car." Watch him closely. He will take the bait—hook, line and sinker. I repeat, all you have to do is _look defeated_.

Now you question him, because you have already confirmed that this is the only thing standing between you and your customer purchasing the automobile. Once again you take the blame, "Just to clarify my thinking sir, why do you feel that the price of this car is so unaffordable?"

Now you shut up. There are three possible outcomes if you hold your tongue. First of all, you will find out if this is his real objection—whether it is prejudice or fact. Secondly, as he explains it to you, he is hooked in even deeper. You must have an answer to his objection, because if you do not, you are in real trouble. So he explains himself and hooks himself even further, or as he explains it, the real objection pops out. You must have the answer to whatever objection pops out. And third, in the process of trying to explain it, it will sound stupid even to him. Many times I have been in this very situation and all of the sudden the prospect will look at me and say, "Okay, you've got the order," because his own words did not even make sense to him. He has told me this is the only thing standing in the way of giving me his order. He has given "rock-solid" commitments that he cannot go back on. Where does he go from here?

In another scenario, let us say that he reconfirms himself to his objection. What do you do? You answer his objection as I have shown you in chapter six. You must have effective methods for handling his objections. You may reduce it to the ridiculous and get him to admit that fifty cents an hour or one penny per minute (less than the cost of a package of gum) does not really impact him, and his family will have the car they really want instead of the one they are forced to settle for. Let him make an ego decision. And you certainly confirm it by saying, "Now that completely covers that doesn't it, sir?"

With your goal in mind, you hand him your simple agreement, which is attached to a clipboard along with your pen, and say, "Will you simply okay this for me?" or "Will you authorize this agreement?" Believe me, this works! If you are a good enough actor to look defeated, he will keep his word and authorize the purchase order. You have removed everything standing between you and the order, and he has confirmed it. Once you do this, you have the right to ask for and expect to get the order. If you are a real pro, you might insert the *secondary question close* by giving your prospect an *alternative of choice*: "Did you want to use your pen or mine?" Generally, when people are given an alternate of choice, they choose a minor alternate. In this case the choice isn't whether they will purchase or decline but simply how they will authorize the purchase order which closes the sale.

13. The "I'll Think It Over" Close

The greatest single objection in the sales business is, "I'll think it over." First of all, who are you to tell somebody that they cannot take time to think something over? This will completely defeat you unless you master this close. And, *believe me*, they will sell this to you. They will tell you that they made a pact signed in blood that they would never make a major purchase without taking twenty-four hours to consider it or that they have to pray about it. They will swear to you that if you will just come back tomorrow they will give you the order because for whatever reason, they cannot make a decision right now. This is a situation that beats salesmen to death.

> **Transform "I'll think it over" from an objection to a closing opportunity.**

To convert this objection to a closing opportunity, you simply say, "That's fine, sir... Obviously you wouldn't take this time to think it over unless you were really interested, would you? And in all sincerity (you will have to have mastered being sincere), I know you're not telling me this to get rid of me. So may I assume that you're going to give this very careful consideration?" Now he thinks you are going to let him go. It sounds like it, doesn't it? He thinks, "This is great. This guy is going to let me go. He's going to eat all those commitments I gave to him." So he says, "Yeah," he will give it very careful consideration.

Now you set the hook. "As you can see, this is how I make a living and feed my family. May I ask you one question? What phase of the program do you want to think over, sir? Is it the integrity of my firm? Is it my personal integrity?" What are we doing here? We are actually *summary closing* him. Do you remember the summary close? You will say, "Is it this? Is it that? Is it this? Is it that?" and he'll say, "No. No. No. No." All of a sudden he is going to realize what is happening and he is going to stop you and say, "Yeah, that's it! That is the only part I want to think over." Now what do you have? You have a final objection. Now you close on that final objection, and, tell me, where does he go without admitting he is a liar?

> **These closing questions will put dollars in your pocket starting the second you begin to use them.**

You see, the real problem is that he has every right to think it over and you have nothing to get your teeth into. What you must do is take, "I'll think it over," and reduce it to a specific final objection because you can handle the objection, can't you? You cannot handle an intangible objection.

This *I'll think it over close* is great. Normally, when a prospect tells you "I'll think it over," you think in your mind, "Oh, crap. There goes another sale." But when you handle *I'll think it over* in this manner, you will think "Great, fantastic, wonderful," and you will be able to close over fifty percent of the *I'll think it over* objections. But there is one caveat I must give you. There is a point in the close where if you stop for breath, you will blow the whole thing. Can you tell me what that point is? I will tell you. The point where you could blow the whole close if you pause for breath is when you say, "What part of the program is it you want to think over?" If you pause here, he will say, "The whole thing." Then you are dead! You have to say, "What part of the program do you want to think over," and then without pausing, you move directly into the summary question close. "Is it this? Is it that? Is it this? Is it that?" Once you get into that first "Is it…?" you start closing in on him. If you learn to use this close effectively, conversationally, and with skill, when he says, "I'll think it over," you will think, "Great, I got this one!"

One Final Thought

I want to refer back to a close I discussed earlier—the *sharp-angle close*. It is critical in all areas of selling. It is a closing opportunity that is laid in your lap five to ten times a day. Always remember that more orders are lost than you can possibly imagine simply because you *talk too much*. But furthermore, when your prospect asks the question, "Can I get it in green?" and you say, "Yes, you can get it in green," question closing *demands* that you say, "Did you want it in green?" If he says, "Yes," he has bought. If he asks you, "Can I get a three-day delivery?" You should say, "Do you want three-day delivery?" If he says, "Yes," he has bought.

> **Unless you add the magic of action with practice, you will remain an order-taker.**

If she says, "Do you have ruby red lipstick?" and you say, "Yes," you have blown it! You must say, "Do you want ruby red lipstick?" How many of these closing opportunities have you missed every day of your life in every field of selling, from multi-level marketing to real estate or selling cars? Do you see my point? Do you get the message? Do you understand? Wouldn't you agree? Do you follow me? These closing questions will put dollars in your pocket starting the second you begin to use them.

What I have attempted to do is give you basic elemental closing techniques in a simple context that you can begin to use and adapt to your presentation or selling opportunity *immediately*. When I read other legendary sales trainers' books which may be four hundred pages long, I found that most of the closing techniques were adaptations of J. Douglas Edwards' basic closes. This is why I feel that if you take these closing elements and adapt them to your presentation as they fit, you will begin to increase your income toward that seven-figure goal—and immediately! Remember, the entire sales process is a *sequential* close from the moment you open your mouth.

If you review your actions, I bet that you can think of five situations you have missed today, or at least this week. I have attempted to give you J. Douglas Edwards' simple formulas which you can adapt to any presentation. But unless you add the *magic of action with practice* and actually use these closes, you will remain an order-taker or a sales clerk and miss being part of the greatest and most magical profession in the world.

> **The entire sales process is a *sequential* close from the moment you open your mouth.**

Now that I have introduced you to the closes that helped make me and many others such successes, I hope I have only whetted your appetite for your own sales increases. I hope I have instilled in you a desire to be the most amazing professional sales artist that your prospects have ever dealt with. Remember, they have done business with thousands of salespeople, but they have never met anyone like *you*. If you are committed to being the best, it's time to take the next step: advanced closing!

Edward Harding

CHAPTER 8

Advanced Closing

Have you started doing the work necessary to commit the closes from the previous chapter to memory—to being second nature? If so, you are showing a true commitment to professionalism. Now you're ready for your next lesson—*advanced* closing. The most important thing you will realize when you get into advanced closing is that you are no longer ashamed of being a salesman. Any close delivered professionally and with true creativity is advanced.

These days I see many more women than I used to who are great professional closers—many times better than men—because they have a burning desire to be great. This is due to the fact that they have been suppressed underneath the glass ceiling for so long. Today you hear of women who are CEOs of major corporations. The first one who comes to mind is Carly Fiorina, the ex-CEO of Hewlett Packard who ran for the U.S. Senate against incumbent Barbara Boxer.

Unfortunately she lost, but it showed just how far a professional such as Carly Fiorina could go. You could see the sparkle in her eyes, and you could sense her spirit even on television. The interesting thing is that if you had asked her mother when she was an infant what she would like her daughter to become, she probably would have said a wife and mother. While wives and mothers are fantastic, the idea of her becoming involved in sales and becoming the CEO of a giant multi-national corporation would probably never have come to mind. And remember, she can also be a wife and mother.

Having hired hundreds of successful women, I have always said that the only difference between a man and a woman is the ability to bear a child and a few hormones. But when it comes to our minds, they are the same. An intelligent brain is a brain, whether it belongs to a man or a woman. What is important and what may differ is what you *do* with your brain.

When you walk tall in the profession of selling, advanced closing becomes almost automatic. Your dignity and spirit radiate because, in actuality, advanced closing begins the moment you open your mouth and begin to get the critical commitments and assumptive tie-downs that lead to the close throughout the entire presentation. You also learn to eliminate objections during your presentation rather than dealing with them at the end. You develop a *closing instinct* which guides you to the point of the sale when you *get the order*!

The "What Do You Think, Honey?" Close

An example of an advanced close is the *"What do you think, honey?" close.* This is for those of you who sell to couples. Assume you are dealing with a couple named Bob and Mary. You may be selling insurance in the home, or you may be selling furniture on commission in a large furniture store or in your own store. What happens here is that, at the point of sale, one party turns to the other and says, *"What do you think, honey?"*

When you hear one of them say, "What do you think?" whether it is Bob or Mary, that person is sold.

For example, Bob turns to Mary and says, "What do you think, honey?" You must immediately, tactfully, and politely interrupt and say, "What do you think, Bob? Do you like…?" When he says, "Yes," that he likes it, it is you and Bob against Mary. It is two against one. Mary may hem and haw, but ultimately she will agree that if he likes it, she will go along with him.

Getting back into the flow, you simply hand your order blank or agreement, whichever it is, to *Mary* and say, "All I need is your okay or authorization right here." Point to the dotted line and hand Mary your pen. Why do I say to hand your pen to *Mary*? The reason is because Mary just said that she would go along with Bob, and once you have her authorization, his authorization is *automatic*. (As a point of interest, nine times out of ten, you will find that Mary makes the buying decisions in the family and handles the checkbook. This is why it is so important that during your great presentation you may want to focus equal energy on Mary as you do on Bob.)

Here is one point of caution. *It takes guts* to interrupt and say, "What do you think, Bob?" But you must do this tactfully, diplomatically, *and immediately*, or you will lose your timing and it will look contrived. Remember, nothing must ever look contrived. Your words must be conversational in nature. They must flow with enthusiasm and sincerity.

I want to add that this close also works if you have a prospect who brings along a friend. Always work the friend. He will persuade your prospect.

The Big Tipper Close

This close works great when you have a product designed for Mary's use and enjoyment but Bob is just not going along. Let us say, for example, you are selling a vacuum cleaner in the home for $1,200, which works out to about $40 a month or a $1.50 a day. Like I said, by giving a great presentation, you have earned the right to walk out of that house with the order in your pocket.

The *big tipper close* is designed to bring Bob around—and hard. You want to bring him around *really* hard. In other words, if he does not go along, he'll be sleeping on the couch for the next month, or you will be leaving the house as Bob and Mary scream at each other.

Here is how it works. You turn to Bob and say, "Are you a big tipper, Bob?" Bob will smell a trap and will *not* say, "Yeah, I'm a big tipper." He will probably say, "No, I'm just an average tipper." You say, "Great. What would you say the average tip is today, 15% or 20%, Bob?" He will say, "Fifteen." Now you say, "Bob, when you take the family to dinner, how much is the average check, $50 to $100?" Thinking he is one step ahead of you, Bob will say, "We go out for the dinner special at Denny's, and the check is about $40." Now you have him locked in. He is in serious trouble. You say, "Great! That means that you would leave a $6.00 tip, right?" He says, "Right."

> **How would you like the key to unlocking unlimited income?**

Now you say, "Bob, just to clarify my thinking, you're telling me that you will give a perfect stranger $6.00 for serving you one meal. Mary serves you breakfast, lunch and dinner; she transports and takes care of your children as well as keeping your house beautiful. Don't you think Mary is worth $1.50 a day so that your family can have an even more immaculate home?"

Immediately place the agreement in front of Bob and say, "Bob, just okay this for me right here. And tell Mary you love her and want to make her job as a wife and mother easier." Can you imagine what will happen if he refuses? This one is a killer. If Bob says, "No," Mary will *kill* him. This close was given to me by Dan Vega.

Plenty More

These two advanced closes are only examples. It is my goal to keep this book short and simple so you can read and understand it easily. But I will tell you that every product in every different company will have its own set of product-related advanced closes. I suggest you learn them as well as expanding your professional knowledge by studying other great teachers such as Brian Tracy, Tommy Hopkins, and Tony Robbins.

I will tell you a funny story. When I was new in sales, my mentor, Joe, was running a sales meeting and was training salesmen. I thought I would be a wise guy and stump him. I gave him what I thought was an impossible objection. He looked at me with steely eyes and said that he would force me to say, "Yes." The only caveat was that I could not admit that I was a liar, and I could not throw him out of my house. He proceeded to box me into a corner by asking questions related to the pivotal commitment, and I could not renege on my commitment without admitting that I lied.

> **Most people give up five minutes before the miracle.**

When he was finished with me, I was forced to say, "Yes." I thought, "Damn, I have got to learn how to do that," and I did! I also trained many others to do the same, which I will explain in the next chapter.

You have been given the tools you need to be the number one salesperson with your company. If you are practicing them and applying them, your income is growing. But you are just one person. You must eat and sleep, and you need time for your family. If you are on commission—which is the *only* choice—how do you make money when you are not selling? How would you like the key to unlocking unlimited income?

Really, it's simple—you must duplicate yourself. It's time to learn how to train others…and to make money from their growth and development as professional sales artists. But first, I must cover an essential part of closing that I purposely saved for last.

The Button Up!!!

I have saved the *button up* for the last, but not the least, area of advanced closing.

The reason is that the *button up* is not really a close. It is the point where you have already completed the process and the order is written and packed up in your sales kit. There is no question that you have given a great presentation, closed the sale, and your prospect has authorized or okayed the agreement. All your paperwork is finalized, assuming, of course, that your company has given you a qualified lead. In fact, you took steps during your pre-talk to make sure that no condition existed. As far as you are concerned, this one is in the bag … right? Wrong!!!

The reason this is true is because there is a factor that may take place once you have moved on to your next appointment but prior to delivery of the product. At some point unbeknownst to you, your new customer may either think or talk himself into a very negative state of mind called *buyer's remorse*. When the particular product is delivered, your customer either cancels on delivery or sends it back. All this negative energy manifests itself while you are not present. Therefore, you have no opportunity to prevent it from happening.

Many salespeople who have just completed a vigorous training class lasting at least a week are now ready to charge into the field. They are excited and extremely enthusiastic. In fact, their enthusiasm for the newness of the challenge far outweighs the 6th step of successful selling, which is sincerity. Although you did not ignore sincerity entirely, a bond of trust was created which allowed you to get the order in the first place. Unfortunately, that bond was not strong enough to transcend the negative energy caused by the attack of **buyer's remorse**, which can be very strong and may give the prospect a sense of relief.

Would you like to have a method to diminish or even prevent this from happening?

I can testify to the danger resulting from buyer's remorse. I can relate to the crushing negativity that I have experienced in my own sales career. Many times this horrible feeling brought me to the brink of giving up.

Remember, it's a fact that most people give up five minutes before the miracle. Why does this happen?

The answer is that the strength of character necessary to survive is not a character trait that we are born with. The "I will survive!" attitude is learned. This is why it is so important to have a great teacher, role model, or mentor.

Buyer's remorse is simply another problem, and every problem has a solution. The question is whether you are going to invest all of your energy into the problem–or into the solution. It's really very simple. Are you part of the problem or part of the solution? I am redundant here for emphasis!

One great teacher of metaphysics, Emmet Fox, analogizes the situation very simply. Let's say you have two balloons. The first balloon has "problem" written on it. The second balloon is labeled "solution." If you blow up the first balloon, it gets larger and larger. The same result occurs if you blow up the second balloon. If you put all your air into the first balloon, the problem becomes larger. If you blow up the second balloon, the solution becomes larger and larger. In which would you choose to invest your precious breath? This is universal law and will become part of your core belief system.

> The "I will survive!" attitude is learned. It's not something you're born with.

In my life, my mentor, Joe Martin, taught me to look at the alternatives. At age twenty-seven with a high school education, I was not headed to medical school to become a doctor; nor was I on my way to law school, and so on down the list of possible high income occupations. Lastly, I was certainly not becoming a rock star nor a movie star, many of whom ended up broke anyway because they never learned about business or how to invest. I'll cover this extraordinary strength in chapter 12.

When I followed my mentor's direction and examined my alternatives, I realized that I could achieve and master the profession of sales—or I could pump gas or stock shelves in a market.

Know that I have been intentionally repetitious because this is so important! It can make you or break you when that moment of crucial decision comes.

Back to buyer's remorse...I had no choice but to invest all my energy into solving the problem! I had to project myself "back to the future" understanding that as part of human nature, some level of remorse would take place when my presence no longer existed in the immediate environment of my prospect and he was out of my control. My job was to psychologically keep my prospect in the same mental state.

> **I tried to imagine how I could make my personal power remain after I had left.**

I had to solve the problem using all the tools I had been given. I tried to imagine how I could make my personal power remain after I had left. As I reflected and meditated, the tiny voice clearly created the revelation that my answer lay in the 6th step of successful selling: sincerity combined with using the psychological strategy of obligation.

As I was saying goodbye to my prospect, I had to make the bond of sincerity extend into the future. I thanked my new friend and customer for the courtesy and goodwill he had shown me. I acknowledged my feelings that, not only had I created a mutually beneficial new business relationship, I had also made a friend for years to come.

Now I had to put the "writing in stone." The best way to do this was to actually take the "bull by the horns." I told my new friend there was one thing I had to cover before I left. I said to him that to the best of my ability, I had answered all of his questions. And if there was any doubt remaining, I surely hoped he would tell me now.

The reason I say this is that if I were to bring in an order that was not properly explained, or if I had left any issue unclear, my boss would "have my head." Most importantly, I wanted to make sure I had done a good job. I explained to him that this is how I made my living and fed my family, so before I left, I wanted to make sure that I had done my job well and that *he would not change his mind tomorrow*. When he replied in the affirmative, I sincerely stated, "I believe a man's word is his bond. Let's shake hands on it."

> **The *button up* is pure sincerity and trust. It must be accomplished with heartfelt diplomacy and tact.**

Please be advised that the *button up* is pure sincerity and trust. It must be accomplished with heartfelt diplomacy and tact. You must use the 6th step of successful selling, sincerity, as a true professional.

If you make a mistake, instead of creating the armor that will protect you from remorse, you may instead plant a doubt; then the process backfires on you!

Nine out of ten times, this sincere, honest approach will lock in your order like steel. The very simple reason is that most people are good people who will follow through with you and keep their word. Do you understand what I am saying? Do you have the dignity, honor, and integrity to make this work for you?

Bet your career on it!

Edward Harding

Chapter 9

Recruiting and Training: In Order to Keep it, You Have to Give it Away

This chapter relates to universal and natural law. It is also the secret and the key to the Holy Grail of sales, *the override*, which comes from getting paid a commission on every sale made by each person you have hired and trained.

The override system in sales is what opens the door to unlimited income. This is where you not only get all the toys, houses, cars, boats, and private planes, but you also have the opportunity to become a teacher and share what you have gained with others. There is an old saying: "If you give a man a fish, you feed him for a day. If you teach him *how* to fish, you feed him for life." This brings us to one of the spiritual and most gratifying giving activities in the sales business because now you become a teacher.

> **The override system in sales is what opens the door to unlimited income.**

Earlier I spoke of successful people. I used examples such as teachers and nurses. Normally these occupations do not lead to unlimited income. In sales, you get the best of both worlds. You get to be a teacher, and you get the opportunity to become wealthy. Aside from absorbing the steps needed to become a professional, this is the most important lesson you will learn in the sales business. I will give you a pragmatic example of how you exponentially increase your income by not only learning this lesson but also by putting it into action.

Sharing The Wealth...By Teaching Others To Make It

> **If you want to reach the highest level of your profession, you must learn to give it away.**

Let us say that you have reached your peak as a professional salesman selling a high commission product. You are earning a pre-tax income of $250,000 a year. If you hire ten people and train them each to do 75% of the volume that you do, you will have increased your overall team's production by 750%. That means that each member of your team will be earning at least $180,000 per year. Your override on their production should be at least 5% of what they make. So if you have ten people who make $180,000 a year, and you make 5% (which is $9,000 times 10), you make an additional $90,000 a year or a pre-tax total of $340,000. That is from teaching ten people to do what you do!

Now let us *really* talk about some numbers. If you do as I did, you can receive overrides on five hundred salespeople. Let us say that the five hundred salespeople have an average income of $80,000 a year. At that level, your override is 2%, or $800,000 a year. Add that to the $250,000 you are earning yourself and you will be making over $1 million a year—pretty close to $100,000 a month pre-tax income. This is what I did, and believe me, when you earn that kind of income, you very quickly convert from a liberal to a conservative because you want to keep what you have earned! In Chapter 12 we will talk about what you *do* with that income and more importantly how that income can work for you.

Want To Keep It? Learn To Give It Away

Here we assimilate the universal law of giving. If you want to reach the highest level of your profession, you must learn to *give it away*. A small, petty mind may think that in training others he is going to create competition for himself. This is untrue because everyone you train will be on your team and will look to you for guidance and instruction. What you are actually doing is *giving yourself a promotion*. Now you are a sales manager, and you must not only think like a professional salesman, you must learn to think like a manager, a leader.

How do you recruit? One simple way is when you pull into Starbucks in your Mercedes and observe that young guy or girl sitting and drinking coffee, you simply ask them if they would like to drive a Mercedes, like yours. When they say, "Yes," you give them your card and say, "Call me." That is a very simplistic method of recruitment, but I must say, it is not as effective as others.

The best method I have seen for recruiting young, energetic, educated people is to run a blind ad that states: "Manager trainee," and offer a significant but not ridiculous amount of money. Instruct the ad reader to call your number and ask for you by name. I have run these ads all over the United States and have had mass interviews of anywhere from 20-100 people at a time.

> **Help your salespeople forget their fear of selling on commission.**

During the interview, conduct a mini-motivational seminar to get them excited about the product and enthusiastic about the money. Help them forget their fear of selling. Make it look easy. After all, it is a sequential close. By the time you begin to teach them to become professionals, they are already making money. Many companies today offer draws against commission. In my day, there were no draws. They hired them in masses, trained them in classes, and kicked them in their asses. The cream would float to the top. That is exactly how I gave Tony Robbins his first job. He actually quit his senior year of high school to work for me. As I mentioned earlier, he said he could learn more from me than he could in high school. He has succeeded beyond his wildest dreams and helped many people.

Another method of recruiting is advertising for a particular type of individual and conducting one-on-one interviews. This way you will learn more about a person as you speak privately. I never really liked individual interviews as I found them too time consuming. I could get much better results running a mass interview and separating the wheat from the chaff as I went along.

> **If you want to reach for the stars and earn unlimited income, you must give other people opportunities.**

There are many creative means of recruiting. I have seen multi-level marketing companies that had large social events as well as bumper stickers and signs saying, "If you want to get rich, ask me how." Different companies have also used caps, pins, jackets, and other apparel. Big ticket advertisements for recruiting include billboards, bus stop benches, radio ads, infomercials, and cable television ads. Both marketing and recruiting today have been greatly enhanced by the use of websites, the internet, and other forms of media. In fact, there are dedicated websites offering everything from recruiting to seminars. It is a whole new world on the Internet. You are only limited by your own creativity. This is also the method Joe Martin used to recruit me. He simply bought me a drink and had it sent over to me. When I offered to reciprocate, he told me that he was going to a different establishment but I could join him a little later—which I did. That movement gave him control of me. He kept me with him for about three days, including flying me across country first class. But the moment I walked into his house, he really had me. When I saw the white marble entry with the large yacht in front, I wanted what he had. You might think that these are extreme measures to hire one individual, but I made him millions and millions of dollars.

I will conclude this chapter by reminding you that if you want to reach for the stars and earn unlimited income, you *must* give other people opportunities. You *must* then follow through by caring enough to offer the best training to those who trust you. The phonies and the cons will not build a company. You must be real; you must sincerely want to help people succeed. And by the way, it gives you tremendous personal satisfaction, too, as well as unlimited earning potential.

Helping others by learning to share what you have learned is incredibly important. It's the key to going beyond yourself—not just what you can sell alone, but also by tapping what the power of giving can do inside of you. All of this bears on the philosophy of selling which is so important to understand at our deepest level. Read on and I will explain the most important element of sales as a philosophy.

CHAPTER 10

The Philosophy of Successful Selling

The philosophy of successful selling can be summed up in three words: *service, service, service*. You must have an attitude of service. It will help you build your own enthusiasm as well as the sincerity that it takes to make people believe in you.

Years ago, I knew a real estate salesman who succeeded beyond his own wildest expectations because, in his mind, he was doing God's work, helping people to find homes. In fact, he became so successful that, sadly, his motivation changed from an attitude of being of service to one of greed. As a result, he decided to open a nightclub. He lost the very principle that made him wealthy and exchanged it for lust, excitement, or greed. He became so cocky and spent a fortune on this nightclub with its high dollar lease payments. It was not a successful venture. In the end, he was broke.

> **The philosophy of successful selling can be summed up in three words: service, service, service.**

Funny things happen as you begin to experience success as a professional. When you began, you were humble and eager to learn. When you become successful and start making money, people begin to seek you out for your ideas and experience. They will copy you. You will become a leader, or, as Tony Robbins calls the process, "unleashing the giant within." You will go into restaurants and bars where maitre d's and waiters will bow to serve you for those generous tips. You will find that you attract members of the opposite sex who want to plug into that positive energy—or should I say "hook up." You will look better because you dress better. You may even have that Rolex watch, BMW, or summer home.

The Rise Of The Ego

All of these wonderful things can have an overriding effect; they bring out the *ego*. Once ego appears, look out! We can erroneously take on an attitude of: "Don't you know who I am?" Arrogance prevails, and before you know it, bad things start to happen. The seven deadly sins—pride, sloth, lust, greed, envy, gluttony, and anger—begin to manifest themselves in your behavior. This is all a result of your ego taking control. This has happened to me many times; I was not smart enough to learn the first time. But I eventually learned this secret.

> **When you lose the desire to be of service, your whole attitude is off-center.**

The important thing to remember is that when you lose the desire to be of service to your prospects, as well as those who work for you, your whole attitude is off-center. How long you remain off-center is up to you. I have found that I can center myself with a couple of minutes of meditation. Focus on the spirit that helped you succeed. This is called getting *back to basics*. Every super-successful person I have ever known has experienced the exact pattern of behavior that I have described, but they have pulled themselves back to their center before they created total destruction. Actually, some did create total destruction…and had to start all over again. But most of them remembered their basic core beliefs and succeeded again. Practice universal harmony in your life on a daily basis. Remember, the definition of a leader is "a trusted servant."

Positive And Negative Traits

In my experience, I have found that one of the characteristics of successful people is their obsessive-compulsive personality—to one degree or another. Some people become so driven that they wind up *dead*. Others, who have real core beliefs, can pull themselves back from the brink of disaster. These obsessions can include the desire to make money, compulsive work habits, substance abuse, or a lack of core values.

False pride is really dangerous because many times false pride cannot see or recognize itself. You have to recognize when you have made a mistake; you must possess the humility to admit it. Only then can you correct it.

Another dangerous obsession, as I have found in my own life, is anger. Initially I thought anger was just another form of energy I could use in a positive manner. In the beginning it worked. Ultimately I found myself *addicted* to my anger. I actually got high being angry. As a result, I destroyed many relationships. When I realized the destructive part anger played in my life, I was determined to get rid of it. My method was to give it to God. Gratefully, I gave it away many years ago, day by day, and today I have very little anger. Sure, I get angry when people try to abuse me, but I do not carry it around. I let my feelings be known; if I am right, I am right; and if I am wrong, I apologize and pay the nickel.

What Really Matters

That pretty much gives you a little of the wisdom I have gained over forty years in the sales profession. I have had ups and downs. As of today, I would say that I am doing pretty well. I have a good relationship with my wife, who is the love of my life. I have two great children: my oldest daughter, Victoria, is in her first year of law school as I write this. I hope she will be a great attorney. My youngest daughter, Grace, who is sixteen years old is the editor of her school newspaper, student body vice president, and has a 4.17 grade point average. She is a great source of pride to me. She runs with me—maybe I should say she "jogs" with me, although she is much faster than I am. She ran her first mile at four years old! I love them both, and they both love me. They are what is really important.

The important motto that I live by is *the second I get cocky, I start going downhill*. I know this from experience; it is not up for discussion. As a result, I have learned to put my ego in my pocket in one second. By doing this and *stepping out of myself*, I manage to stay centered simply because I cannot accept the alternatives…and believe me, I have seen the alternatives.

> **The important motto that I live by is the second I get cocky, I start going downhill.**

In the last two chapters we talked about giving and the life philosophy of sales. These things are vital elements to add to your life if you wish to transcend from being a salesperson who simply makes money into being the kind of giving, centered individual who can be a true and lasting success. And while these things are very important, I want to give you some concrete tools for creating success. In the next chapter, we will take a few moments to talk about setting goals. This is the only way in which you can channel and direct your desire for success into tangible, repeatable results.

Chapter 11

Setting Goals

This is another short but important chapter simply because it will give you direction. I was just listening to a tape made in 1956 by Earl Nightingale called *The Strangest Secret*, which I told you about earlier. In it, he talks about the difference between a success and a failure. A success is a person who is working toward a worthwhile goal. What is a worthwhile goal? According to Mr. Nightingale, it is "the progressive realization of a worthy ideal."

Mr. Nightingale uses the example of a ship that sets out to sea with a pilot and a destination. The pilot charts the course for that ship toward its destination. About 99% of the time, that ship will reach its destination successfully. Contrarily, if you take a ship and put it out to sea with no destination and no pilot, that ship will ultimately wind up on the rocks, a failure.

You become what you think about.

Why is this analogy significant? Setting a goal gives you a destination. If you work faithfully, you will reach that destination. In other words, what the mind can conceive, the body can achieve. You will achieve your goal. I have listened to this particular tape literally thousands of times. I understand that the strangest secret is not really strange and is not really a secret. It is very simple: *You become what you think about.*

The dominant thoughts of your mind reproduce themselves. If the dominant thoughts of your mind are negative, you will achieve negative results. *If the dominant thoughts of your mind are positive, you will achieve positive results.*

> **I made long-term goals my destination and short-term goals my immediate rewards.**

This is why goal setting is so important. If you set a worthy goal and you constantly think about that goal, you will ultimately elevate your entire thought process. Think about it—every day your mind is constantly bombarded with impulses, one-second thoughts, or mental pictures. In today's world, many of these impulses—such as unemployment, recession, war, and fear—are negative. If you focus on these negative impulses, you will certainly get negative results in your day-to-day life.

The question is, how do you get rid of this negativity? The secret is that whenever you catch a negative thought passing through your mind, immediately replace it with a picture of your positive, worthy goal. This is a process called *visualization*. You visualize yourself living the life you sincerely want to live. Keep that picture in your mind. Write it down and keep it where you can see it constantly. I put notes on my mirror and on the refrigerator door. Keep them on your desktop or in your notebook.

I have a great lifestyle. I spend the winter in Palm Springs, which has the most beautiful climate in the world during winter months. In the summer, I live at the beach and spend a lot of time on my boat, which is not really a boat—it is an 80-foot yacht. People ask me, "How did you achieve this great life?" I tell them, "I painted a picture in my mind and moved into it."

Does this mean that it happened overnight? Did I create the picture and instantly move into it? The answer is no. I painted the picture in my mind, and through the years, I set long-term goals and short-term goals. A long-term goal can be a new home. A short-term goal can be a new suit. My first goal in sales in 1969 was to make $300 a week. When I achieved that goal, I immediately set another goal. You must do this the minute you achieve your goal! Set a new one, only make it greater! When I learned about long-term and short-term goals, I made long-term goals my destination and short-term goals my immediate rewards. This process has worked for me for over four decades. If it will work for me, it will work for you. But you must really follow the plan, set the goals, and have a deep-seated belief that you will achieve. In other words, *plan your work, and work your plan.*

> **Plan your work, and work your plan.**

The Thirty-Day Test

In Napoleon Hill's book, *Think and Grow Rich*, and in Earl Nightingale's tape, *The Strangest Secret*, they speak about a 30-day test. As I touched on before, this means that for thirty days you think nothing but positive thoughts, visualize your goals, and see yourself achieving those goals.

Everybody wants something, and everybody is afraid of something. Write down on a card the thing you want more than anything else in the world. It can be anything: a new home, a better relationship, more money, a baby, a promotion, wisdom, joy, or any other goal that is important to you. On the other side of the card, write the message from the *Sermon on the Mount*: "Ask and ye shall receive. Seek and ye shall find. Knock and it shall be opened unto you." Put this card in your wallet and take it out and look at it several times a day. Remember to think positive thoughts for thirty days.

Sounds simple, doesn't it? Here is the catch. If you find yourself overwhelmed by negativity, anger, fear, frustration, or any other negative emotion, you must immediately start the 30-day test all over again. As I said earlier, it took me fifteen years to pass it. It is not easy. But your life will progress in a positive manner simply by *attempting* to pass the test. Just remember to replace any negative creeping thoughts immediately with a mental picture of living in your goals.

That is why I made goal setting its own chapter in this book. Any person working toward a worthy goal and really believing that he can achieve what he believes in will become more and more successful. As strange as it sounds, achieving a goal is anti-climactic because you immediately have to set a new one. But the great secret is to keep positive thoughts forefront in your mind and to *enjoy the journey.*

Now you have more information on the value of goals. You can order *The Strangest Secret* from Nightingale-Conant on the internet. You can also buy *Think and Grow Rich* at any bookstore if you haven't already. Remember, great ideas are nothing without action. *Action is the magic word. So take action.* Order that CD and buy that book. They will lead you to other teachers who will help you on your path to peace of mind. Ultimately, *peace of mind* is your goal; without it, you have nothing. I have known people with all the money in the world who did not seek "peace of mind" while "enjoying the journey" as their ultimate goal. These people not only missed out on the joy of life, but they often self-destructed–sometimes fatally.

> **Great ideas are nothing without action.**

Visualize your goals. See yourself achieving and progressing. Ultimately, the thought process will become a part of your subconscious mind. This subconscious powerhouse will help create your own personal miracle.

Chapter 12

The Art of Selling Creates Money: What Do We Do With The Money?

"To be or not to be—that is the question."
William Shakespeare

There are different stages in the life of a salesperson. There is the beginning when we learn the craft. There are the intermediate stages when we experience various levels of success (and possibly failure). Then there are the last stages when we have reached the goals we set for ourselves and, in many cases, exceeded them. Nobody wants to stay stuck at the same level. We should all attempt to reach that impossible dream. Dream big! Give 110%; achieve more than you ever believed you could. Accomplish the impossible!

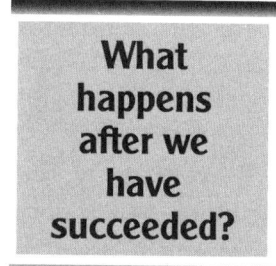

> **What happens after we have succeeded?**

But that brings us to an important question. What happens after we have succeeded? What then? As you are reading this book, you have probably attempted to reach a certain level of success. You may have moved into the picture of the house that you painted in your mind, whether it is owning your first or second home, a condo in Vale, a home at the beach, in L.A. or in any part of the world where you might chose to dwell. My friend realized his vision of a New York brownstone overlooking Central Park. As you progress, you will fulfill the youthful pictures of accumulating toys and superficial stuff, including cars, clothes, jewelry, and maybe a couple of ex-wives.

> **You must self-educate in order to make your business practices more sophisticated.**

You must self-educate in order to make your business practices more sophisticated. You will learn of different entities, different types of corporations, family trusts, family limited partnerships, and other structural opportunities. In today's litigious society, asset protection is *critical*. It is also important that you discover estate planning as early in life as possible so that you can create the correct structures as you begin to build wealth.

I didn't do this. Of course, I was kind of busy, but I am *paying the price today* to catch up and learn what I should have known as I started to accumulate properties. Don't be sucked into schemes by fast-talking con artists who offer disreputable tax evasions. Have a trusted mentor refer you to attorneys and accountants who are brilliant and who possess an attitude of service while keeping your best interest at heart.

Always hire the best! They may cost a little more, but they are definitely worth it in the long run. As an example, the American government has created a horrible tax called the "death tax," which takes 55% of your wealth from your children. (This truly unethical idea double-taxes money because you have already paid State and Federal Income Tax on it as you earned it.) Here we have the theft of your ability to create your own family dynasties as other wealthy families have done in the past. I will repeat this because it is important. Any wealth you may have accumulated is decimated and stolen from your family because 55% of it goes to the government upon your demise.

This is definitely not the America that revolted from England with events such as the Boston Tea Party. Again, here I get into an area of political correctness because this information is not for socialists, liberals, or progressives whose goal is to redistribute wealth; rather it's for those who want to build great American families. Remember, in the words of James Taylor, "teach your children well." Motivate them to think straight and not be influenced by those in today's society who promote a lifestyle of neurotic celebrities, unruly sports figures, and other false idols who create a superficial culture.

I honestly believe it's a fact that if you redistributed all the wealth in the world, in ten to twenty years, the same people would find a way to re-accumulate it *because they know how to create it and make it work for them.* But why waste time? The American culture was built on individual freedom and a person's right to acquire all that he or she could and then to use that to begin taking care of others. You can't give away something that you don't have.

> **If you redistributed all the wealth in the world, in ten to twenty years, the same people would find a way to re-accumulate it.**

I will talk more about this later in this chapter as I expound on the strength and hardiness of the Americans who built this country. It's important to realize that we must not allow ourselves to be "dumbed down" and let our children be taught by various media to worship false gods. I truly believe this is not the culture we want to create for the future of America. The great changes that must be made will be the responsibility of future generations. They are the ones who will be robbed and loaded down with debt and deficits which they will have to work all their lives to repay. It is our responsibility, however, to educate and pass on the principles needed for creating, maintaining and investing wealth.

Edward Harding

All People Evolve At Their Own Pace

In life there is an evolution that takes place as you age. It's different for everyone. I came to a crossroad when I realized that I had to decide what I wanted to be when I "grew up." I had conquered the challenge of making money, which was my original goal. Along the way I evolved as a person, realizing that all of the possessions in the world would not fix the hole in my gut. I discovered that I must learn to set non-material goals that involved taking action on my core beliefs. This is what makes life worth living. In other words, I had to prioritize my values. By age thirty-six I was a multi-millionaire. I had done almost everything there was to do, but there was still something missing.

> **You can't give away something that you don't have.**

My old friend and mentor, Joe Martin, suggested that I consider having a family. I thought that was a good idea, so I got married in 1980. A year later, I was the father of a beautiful baby girl I named Victoria. When I held her in my arms, I experienced something I had never experienced before—a real emotion. Here was this infant completely dependent on me for everything and for everything she would become. I understood that my job as a father was to teach her to think straight. When I realized the scope of responsibility entailed in teaching my daughter, I was elated but humbled by the challenge. It was not until later that I experienced the real challenge, and I must say there were times when I was not so elated. Today, my daughter Victoria is in her first year of law school and she seems excited. I realize it will be a great day in my life when I see her get that bar card. My youngest daughter, Grace, is a constant source of joy. Her accomplishments at such a young age also make me proud of her.

As my life continued to evolve, I realized that I had to learn to invest the money I was making as I grew older so that the money could do the heavy lifting required to maintain my standard of living while leaving something to pass on to my children.

This last chapter is extremely personal, as many of these lessons are those I discovered while I embarked on my own journey. I have many friends who had the same experiences. In fact, many of them I helped and trained. Some of them even exceeded my accomplishments. I found that the evolution and the journey were similar for all of us but we experience them for ourselves and in our own way and time. You will too. I have had to learn to enjoy the journey and stop to "smell the roses," which sometimes is very difficult to do, while I look inside myself for that tiny voice of common sense and God-given direction. During these moments, inspiration will come to enable you to solve problems that baffle others. This will not happen while your mind is racing. You must shut down the "race mind," possibly by meditation. Empty your head of all thought and ego, and you will hear the tiny little voice that speaks very softly.

> By age thirty-six I was a multi-millionaire, but there was still something missing.

Investing

After successfully handling the challenge of "making the money," my next goal was, and yours should be, setting a goal of investing so that hard assets could anchor these accomplishments. It was time to set a new goal: investing the bounty of my efforts. On the face of it, investing may seem like a simple goal. Do not believe that. I never realized how difficult this goal would become. It was definitely a long-term goal. Self-education is paramount. Don't listen to politicians or "get rich quick" salesmen. Look inside yourself; everything you need is inside you, including that tiny voice that comes when your mind is quiet.

The first thing I did was to start studying investments. I read histories of the world's most successful families, including the Astors, the Rothschilds, the Rockefellers and others. What I discovered was that all of these great family fortunes had been built by clever investments in areas of absolute human necessity such as food, health, transportation, housing, communications, and clothing.

> **Investing may seem like a simple goal. Do not believe that.**

I tried to determine where I could fit in. I was not a farmer. I was not a doctor. I was not Howard Hughes. The idea of owning a chain of department stores did not appeal to me. I was not equipped for it, and I did not have the time or the resources to learn from the ground up how to be successful in these different areas of endeavor. During your lifetime, you can learn only a few businesses. If you are really wise, you can master the art of delegating opportunities to other people thereby exceeding the limitations of any one human being.

Some of the great entrepreneurs of our day inherited family businesses that they continued to develop. Rupert Murdoch, for instance, inherited the family business, a newspaper, which, with wise financial controls and business acumen, he turned into the greatest communications empire in existence today. I inherited nothing, but as far back as I could remember, my family had been in the real estate business. My grandfather became president of the Beverly Hills Real Estate Board. With that background, I knew how to buy a house. I also had a special real estate mentor, Earl Morley, Sr. He taught me about investing in income-producing properties.

In 1978 I bought my first rental house. By 1980 I had three rental houses. I wanted to expand my assets by investing in multi-family apartment buildings. I realized that I could be of service and make a profit by providing low cost housing. I believed that just because people are poor does not mean they are bad. I knew I could provide good low cost housing. I discovered that in the real estate market of the early 1980s, most apartment buildings operated with negative cash flows. I definitely did not want to invest in something that was going to lose money. While I would not buy an apartment building that was losing money, I learned that I could *build one* that would make money or, at least, break even while providing appreciation and significant tax advantages.

There is another important aspect of business that cannot be overlooked. It is called *relationships*. You will meet many people on this journey. Some will become life-long friends. We need to nurture and grow these important relationships because they will serve as the basis for our continued growth as both business people and as social beings. I believe that today we call it "networking." Do not overlook these relationships, but be careful. Always associate with people of good character from whom you can learn. Remember, there are many thieves out there networking too. Amazingly, sometimes you may help someone…and later on they will help you!

> **Always associate with people of good character from whom you can learn.**

As I stated, my goal to start a family had been accomplished. We had everything: wonderful holidays, a beautiful home, and an exciting family life. In 1981, I was looking for a larger home for my family. I discovered a fabulous estate built by a general contractor as his own dream house. His name was Joe Price. Unfortunately, he had broken his back in a motorcycle accident, and, after spending eight months in the hospital, that dream house was not capable of accommodating his new physical limitation—e.g. his wheelchair. When I entered his house, every cell in my body screamed, "This is my house." The home was really beautiful. It was a walled estate with an electric gate. The front lawn was one acre of green grass. The long driveway was lined with Queen Anne palm trees, and the entrance to the house was like the entrance to a luxury hotel. You could pull your car into the covered area and enter the beautiful entry hall facing the living room. There was an in-ground, tiled Jacuzzi in the master bedroom, a tennis court, and pool in the rear. The entire west wall of the house was glass, and the view was magnificent. You could see all the way to downtown Los Angeles. It also had a three-car garage.

I made an offer on the property which was well below the asking price. This all took place during the Carter years when home interest rates went as high as 15%. Although he did not accept my offer, he did agree to take my existing home in trade and carry back a second mortgage at a 10.5% interest rate and a payment I could afford. I knew I could beat down his price because he had just spent eight months in a hospital and had a second mortgage coming due. But I decided not to be greedy and grind his price down because I imagined living in the house for many years and could amortize the extra cost over twenty years. I realized that he needed the money more than I did. Because of the fact that I was not greedy and did not push him, we became friends, and his wife, Edna, even babysat my daughter, Victoria.

> **I made one million dollars and got the house for free!**

A year later he was telling me about a piece of property he owned. We could build eleven units on it, but the property was not free and clear. He needed $60,000. I told him I would give him the $60,000. Between the two of us, we could get a construction loan and finish the building. Long story short, I wound up constructing four buildings with him. I made $1 million and got the house for free! That was my entrance into multi-family housing—a miracle! I could not have written that script in my wildest imagination. This happened because I did not squeeze every penny from the purchase of the house.

By 1992 we sold the apartment buildings. I took $3 million and invested it in the Inland Empire just after California's real estate market crashed in the recession of the 1990s. We were able to buy apartment buildings for $10,000 a unit. The best deal we ever made was $7,000 a unit! Compare that with today's market when it costs over $20,000 just for building permits. By 2004, we had almost a thousand units in thirty-five different buildings.

I set the goal in 1978, and twenty-five years later I created a mini real estate empire. I also allowed seven other people to invest with me, not because I needed the money, but because I wanted to help them. You see, the attitude of service enabled me to help friends and family members to provide for their own retirements.

Aware of the unpredictability of business cycles, I set a goal of having my standard of living supported by real estate investments rather than from the sales business. I achieved that goal by 1993.

A New Generation of Entrepreneurs Can Save America

As I write this, I find that we are in the worst economic downturn since the Great Depression of the 1930s. Our government policies are not conducive to business growth. Because of the anti-business atmosphere in America (and California especially), large corporations are outsourcing our jobs to other countries. In California, companies are moving to other states where the atmosphere is business-friendly. Along with the businesses go the jobs. But state and city leaders just don't get it.

Believe me, I understand the necessity of creating a world economy. America cannot be the sole engine driving the new world economy—as it has been for so long. A consequence of our being the "sole engine" in the world is that, since World War II when we rebuilt Japan and Germany, we have been exporting our middle class jobs all over the world. There is so much criticism these days about America consuming too much of the world's energy resources. These one-sided critiques seem to sidestep the fact that if Japan, Korea, Taiwan, India and China couldn't sell their energy consuming automobiles and electronic devices in America, their economies would collapse, as would our own, creating financial Armageddon. You will instinctively know whether or not what I am saying is true.

> **America cannot be the sole engine driving the whole world economy.**

Edward Harding

Let's face it, any country that does not have trading relationships with America is a poverty stricken country. If not for America sharing its wealth with the rest of the world by exporting jobs, the American middle class would still be making watches and refrigerators and washing machines and printers and computers and a whole host of other consumer goods, most of which were invented in the U.S. Would this be a bad thing? Not necessarily; it would just prevent others from making those products in their own countries where they pay only about $1.00 an hour. How can the American labor force compete with these sweatshop pay scales? If we're going to have labor unions, the model should be enforced worldwide in order to create a level playing field and uplift all workers. I understand that this is not immediately possible, but this will eventually take place as it has in Japan.

> **It is time for the younger generations to bring back the values of entrepreneurial America!**

President Barrack Obama and other liberal and progressive thinkers and politicians talk about sharing the wealth. America *has* shared the wealth, and in the process we have impoverished our own middle class and dumbed down our entire society. It is time for the younger generations to bring back the values of entrepreneurial America! We need to build strong people who will build strong businesses because those businesses will become the source of jobs and economic growth for our country and its families in the future. I, along with my wife—who has her own company—have created nearly one hundred jobs that feed almost one hundred families.

As I write this last chapter, I am reminded how tough our American forefathers were. During a period of our history called *Manifest Destiny*, many believed that as the population of people who settled the thirteen colonies grew, America should spread across the entire continent from coast to coast. We completed the Louisiana Purchase with Napoleon III and fought a war with Mexico in order to annex the southwest, including California.

While all this was going on, settlers were crossing America in Conestoga wagons, better known as covered wagons. Tribes of Native Americans repeatedly attacked these groups of settlers. A typical scenario might be that during one of these attacks the father was shot while the mother had to grab the wagon reins not even being able to stop to bury or gather her dead husband. If she stopped, she and her children also risked death—they had to press forward.

I am not trying to stir up political debate with who was attacking whom; my point is that these settlers had to be *unbelievably* hardy, determined, and tough people. I challenge you to walk through a mall, or even a county fair, and ask yourself how many of the people you see would have survived the trials and demands of the early frontier. These were the folks who began the process of building the American Republic into the greatest country to ever inhabit this planet.

> **The challenge of every generation is to use our resources intelligently and to create a new beginning.**

This last chapter, *The Art of Selling Creates Money; What Do You Do With The Money?* is more than just a summary of all we learned in the previous chapters. The challenge to every generation is to use our resources intelligently and to create a new beginning. This will ultimately solve not only the problems of America, but the problems of the *world* while saving the futures of our children.

All Americans must understand that we are blessed to be born in the greatest and wealthiest country that *has ever existed*. We must recognize the conditions and opportunities that still exist here. Just as necessity is the mother of invention, the conditions and opportunities we have in the United States can be the breeding grounds in which we find new solutions to all our problems.

All of my life I have solved real problems. When I ran our direct marketing company, they called me the Fireman, because all I did was fly from one place to another solving problems and putting out fires.

> **You have to solve your own problems by yourself, by looking inside yourself.**

I look at the housing industry today and realize that Fannie Mae and Freddie Mac, the largest home financiers in the world, are *wrecked*. The people responsible for buying mortgages knew they were lending money to people who did not earn enough to repay the loan. Four years later, these culprits walked away with over $100 million in bonuses and left Fannie Mae and Freddie Mac in shambles. *This move ignited the housing crisis, which was the catalyst for the current economic depression.*

It makes me sick when I realize the incompetence that exists at the highest levels of government. Just because these people are part of the "good 'ole boys" network from Harvard, Princeton, or some other Ivy League school, they have gained access to power. Their misuse of that power destroyed opportunities for everyone from the guy with the hammer to the student graduating from college. When I was young, a bachelor's degree meant something and opened doors to greater jobs and better opportunities. Today, a bachelor's degree is a ticket to a minimum wage job. Just last week I went into an Apple store and spoke to a very bright young salesman. He had a master's degree in computer science. I asked him if he were on commission, and he said no. I asked him how much he made; he sheepishly told me $11.50 an hour. I told him to go and get a commission job that would pay him for his education, intelligence, and ability.

Look Inside Yourself For The Solutions

I would like to include in this chapter a line from Donovan Leitch's 1969 hit, *Riki Tiki Tavi*. "Riki Tiki Tavi mongoose is gone; won't be coming around for to kill your snakes no more my love; Riki Tiki Tavi mongoose is gone." The snakes symbolize your problems. The mongoose symbolizes the organizations that would solve problems for us like the United Nations, large organizations, religious institutions, or the government. In the song he says the "mongoose is gone."

You have to solve your own problems by yourself, by looking inside yourself.

Although I wanted this last chapter to be positive, exciting and uplifting, it seems it is a bit scary—if you're unwilling to take *action*. But, *it is still the truth*. The world has problems; we must be the solutions—and we can be!

There is opportunity out there for you, but when you reach the point where you are making money, you must learn to *invest it* wisely. It does not really matter how you make your money. You could be a mechanic or a teacher or a business owner. You can own a garage or a bank. The investment principles are the same. If you start buying rental houses at age twenty-five, by the time you are age fifty-five, they will be paid for. If you own five rental houses and they rent for $2,000.00 a month, you have created a $10,000.00 a month pension that you control, and it cannot be stolen from you. At the same time, you can also provide jobs for your management team.

> **The bottom line is for you to realize that you must invest your money and control your own investments.**

We can learn by watching the pension plans of private companies—as an example, the airlines—being stolen by incompetent people who failed to invest properly in hard assets that produced income. These manipulators managing the pension plans did not earn the money put into these very pension plans—it wasn't their money—so what did they care? Wall Street, limos, Dom Perignon, cocaine, and hookers, along with bad investments, bankrupted most airline pension plans. This contagious disease has gone on to affect the entire structure of private sector pension plans. I wish I had the opportunity to invest that money and protect those senior citizens who worked for thirty plus years and now have nothing to show for it.

Now that you have learned the art of selling, you must also learn the principles of investing. To win at this game, you must plan and enjoy every part of the journey. This final step is crucial: learn to *invest*. As I close this short and simple handbook on selling, the bottom line is for you to realize that you must invest your money and control your own investments.

On A Personal Note...

In concluding this book, I feel that some personal communication with you, my reader, is needed so that you can understand a little bit of what my journey has been like as I traveled from there to here. I turned twenty-one years old in 1964. This was the hippie era, the time of the flower children, the generation that set us free and whose mistakes I can see so clearly now. Of course, hindsight is always 20/20 vision. Fortunately, for me, I dodged many of the bullets I saw other people take. I always seem gifted with the sense of when it was time to quit one activity and move on to another.

I hit the streets of West Hollywood in about 1962 at the age of eighteen. I consider the next nine years my "wasted" years. I had no education and seemed only to want to be hip, slick, and cool. I knew as many people who died from drug overdoses as I knew who died in the Vietnam War.

By 1967, I was fed up with being a bum! One of my pivotal turning points was when I met an attractive young lady in 1967 who agreed to support me. Sounds good, but when we went out the first time, she gave me a ten dollar bill! I immediately experienced a rush of self-loathing that I do not ever recall feeling before. I then made up my mind that I was going to go out and take the first job I was offered. I did, and it turned out to be selling shoes. I hated that job! I told my father that I was too good to sit at people's feet and sell shoes all day. He told me to consider it an apprenticeship. He said that if I did it for two years, I would know everything there was to know about people. It is kind of funny, but it was true.

Today I can look at a person's shoes—the condition, type, wear patterns—and I can generally get an immediate psychological profile of that person. Somewhere along the line my competitive nature kicked in, and I wanted to be the number one salesman in the store. There was a little Jewish guy named Al Goldstein who was a real hustler. He was a funny character about 5'4" with male pattern baldness and a ring of red hair around his head that looked like a Bozo the Clown wig. It took me two years to beat him!

Strangely, as fortune would have it, one night I was sitting with a friend in a Huntington Beach restaurant called *The Whistling Oyster* when I met a guy named Joe Martin. We hit it off, and he took me to his house in Huntington Harbour. I walked into a beautiful, white marble entry hall, and from the living room, I could see a big yacht docked outside his back door.

> **I asked him if he thought I could do what he did. He told me that I didn't have the balls!**

As we talked, he told me that he grew up in an orphanage. I asked him how old he was now; he was thirty-four. I asked him what his net worth was; he told me about $2 million. I asked him if he had inherited the money or made it himself; he made it himself. I asked him what it was he did, and he said that he was an in-home salesman. After spending some time together, I realized that I wanted what he had: a beautiful wife, great home, and kids.

I asked him if he thought I could do what he did. He told me that I didn't have the balls! I asked him to just give me a chance. As it turned out, he owned his own company and gave me a job as a commissioned salesman with the promise that he would give me the best training possible. Joe Martin became my mentor, my best friend, and, years later, my business partner. It was from him that

Edward Harding

I learned that sales was a profession, and I began the process of becoming a *professional*.

We worked together until he passed away at the early age of sixty-three in 1998. We built a nationwide company of which I became the national sales manager, and we opened finance companies. By the time I was thirty-six years old, I was a *millionaire*.

I hired and trained thousands of people all over the country. Many became very successful in a number of different businesses. Over the years I have been privileged to mentor and influence the lives of many young men and women. Most of them—by the time they left—were in better condition than when they arrived. I also helped a couple of friends build very successful sales organizations and invest in real estate.

> **Sometimes the hardest part of getting on the first rung of that ladder is getting through the crowd at the bottom.**

By the time the recession of the 1990s hit, our company was unable to survive, however I was still consulting, hiring, and training for other companies. Fortunately, I sold all my real estate holdings at the peak of the market in about 1989, and by 1992, I was able to start purchasing real estate foreclosures in the Inland Empire of Southern California. By 2004, we accumulated thirty-five properties of various sizes.

And as I sit here today, with God's grace, I gratefully realize that I have managed a 180 degree transformation from the loser of the 1960s. I have a great life, two beautiful daughters of whom I am proud, and a wonderful wife, Paula, who is the love of my life—my true soul-mate and to whom I dedicate this book.

Judging by the results of my living standard today, I would say I turned out a winner. I have been successful in a number of businesses from sales to finance to real estate investment. I feel that the information I am passing on in this book contains a lot of the pragmatism that allowed me to succeed. I believe that anyone who takes the sales methods I describe in this book—and *applies* them effectively—will be able to climb the ladder of success in any business.

Sometimes the hardest part of getting on the first rung of that ladder is getting through the crowd at the bottom. It takes a big action step to do this: casting off the lower behavior and beginning to evolve spiritually, mentally, and physically.

At age sixty-seven, I find myself well-balanced, straight-thinking, and grateful to have lived my life. If I had to do it over again, I would not change a thing. As it turned out, even my shortcomings have allowed me to help other people. I feel that if one person reads this book and it helps him change his life, then it was worth the effort.

Just remember: The difference between a "winner" and a "loser" is a positive or a negative thought. Thanks, God; thanks, Grandad and Grandma; thanks, Dad and Mom; and a special thanks to Joe Martin, a great man with a great heart. And thanks, Paula, for your diligence and dedication.

I wish you all the best,

Edward Harding

"An American Sales Champion"

The Last Word
by Gerald Chamales

You Can — If
You Believe You Can

I met Ed Harding thirty-three years ago and can say, unequivocally, that Ed has been a powerful and positive influence in my life; he was instrumental in both my personal and professional success. He taught me to never give up, to emulate the best practices of winners, and to apply those principles to all aspects of my life. Action and urgency, combined with skill-building and a commitment to excellence in whatever endeavor you pursue, have always been the hallmark of Ed's profoundly life-changing philosophy.

Ed is a "can do" leader who shows his students to "be all that you can be." He teaches that there are no limits other than those that we impose upon ourselves. Think big and develop a burning desire to achieve your dreams, and you can if you believe that you can! That is the message Ed communicates with clarity and conviction based on his own personal transformation as well as the countless people he has helped climb the elusive ladder of success. And the bottom line is that Ed's practical philosophy of personal achievement works!

When I started out in business, I knew very little about how to build my company. Ed was always there to coach and guide me. Ed's message of hope helped me take an actual start-up company, *Rhinotek Computer Products*, from a one-room apartment in Venice Beach, California, with one employee (me) into a business that went from $0 to $58,000,000 per year in sales while employing 250 people in Los Angeles and 400 people in Canada. Ed's success principles enabled me to begin a rapid personal development program that eventually led to *Rhinotek Computer Products* winning the *Ernst & Young Entrepreneur of the Year Award* in 2001 for business service. *Rhinotek's* success was highlighted in a front page article in *The Wall Street Journal* and featured on *CNN, CNBC, Success Magazine, Forbes*, and *The O'Reilly Factor*. Highly lauded was *Rhinotek's* goal to "give back" to our community by hiring the unemployable and giving them skills that enabled over 30% of our work force to come back from the welfare rolls, prisons, work release programs, and halfway houses. Ed Harding's philosophy of personal transformation combined with helping our customers and employees to succeed was the foundation upon which we built *Rhinotek Computer Products* into an industrial and community leader.

In the beginning, I was often frustrated by my lack of experience and knowledge in entrepreneurship. Ed Harding became my "go to" advisor whenever I confronted a business challenge. I often called him daily for counsel. When I had a problem I could not solve on my own, Ed provided a viable, workable solution without hesitation. Ed's positive outlook, his commitment to helping others win, and his extraordinary enthusiasm and energy were instrumental in turning my fears and challenges into winning strategies based on his own personal experiences and wisdom.

Ed Harding is one of the greatest personal motivators I have ever met. He is a true leader in business; he understands the importance of instilling self-discipline, personal initiative, a strategic plan, and strong organizational skills into his students to create lasting cash flow businesses serving their community and employees. As CEO of *Rhinoteck Computer Products,* I hired many Harvard, Wharton, and Stanford MBAs as we built our company. These MBAs made valuable contributions to our growth. However, Ed Harding's success principles were the driving force in *Rhinotek's* foundation of success!

Ed Harding introduced me to Dennis Waitley's *The Psychology of Winning*, Napoleon Hill's *Think and Grow Rich*, and *The Law of Success*, as well as Tony Robbins' *Awaken the Giant Within*. Ed's deep philosophy enabled me to turn my life around from an "almost ran" to a success in business and life. I've also had the privilege of investing with Ed in successful real estate ventures.

Ed is a "world class" entrepreneur and businessman who knows how to make it happen no matter what level of success – or lack of success – you have currently achieved.

In 2006, I successfully exited from *Rhinotek Computer Products*. Today I invest in oil and gas, real estate, films, insurance services, and technology. I am the founder of my own "family office" and use my own capital for a variety of different business opportunities.

…And it all started in that one-room apartment in Venice Beach, California, thirty-three years ago when my friend, Ed Harding, began to spoon-feed me a new philosophy of personal transformation, a new way to think and act, and a belief in the possibilities embedded in the American Dream!

You can confidently take the great philosophy that Ed Harding communicates, and if you act on the "Harding Principles of Success," you will ascend to levels of achievement you never dreamed possible.

All the best,

Gerald "Jerry" Chamales

Equity Value Group

Contact Information

Edward Harding

P. O. Box 2189

Capistrano Beach, California 92624

(888) 511-6827

www.EdwardHarding.com